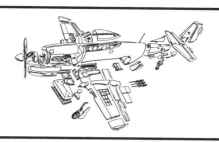

# VOLUME 4

# VOUGHT
# F4U CORSAIR

## By Barrett Tillman

**specialtypress**
PUBLISHERS AND WHOLESALERS

Published by
Specialty Press Publishers and Wholesalers
11481 Kost Dam Road
North Branch, MN  55056
United States of America
(612) 583-3239

Distributed in the UK and Europe by
Airlife Publishing Ltd.
101 Longden Road
Shrewsbury
SY3 9EB
England

ISBN 0-933424-67-1

Designed by Greg Compton

Printed in the United States of America

# TABLE OF CONTENTS

## THE VOUGHT F4U CORSAIR

# PREFACE

Chance M. Vought established a long-lived dynasty of Navy aircraft marked by daring design, bold execution, and wildly erratic success over six decades. The Lewis and Vought Corporation was founded in 1918, and its VE-7 biplane was among the earliest carrier aircraft, operating from USS *Langley* (CV-1) in 1922.

Thus, Vought-Sikorsky Division of United Aircraft Corporation had a long record of Navy business when, on 1 February 1938, the Bureau of Aeronautics proposed a high-performance, single-seat carrier fighter. Based at Stratford, Connecticut, the firm already had built a family of sturdy observation biplanes (the UO series), floatplanes (OS2Us), and scout-bombers (SBUs and SB2Us). However, the company's previous fighter designs for the Navy (FU, XF2U, XF3U) and Army (V-141/143) had gone nowhere. In fact, the Navy fighters proved dead ends or evolved into other types, while the Army entries were based on Northrop designs.

The BuAer letter led to Vought's V-166B. (The V-166A, designed around the P&W R-1830, was never built.) A contract was signed on 11 June, 1938, providing for construction of the XF4U-1, with mockup inspected by BuAer representatives eight months later, in February 1939. First flight came on 29 May 1940, less than two years after the contract date.

Vought's general manager, C.J. McCarthy, appointed a winning design team to work under chief engineer Rex Beisel. The project engineer was Frank Albright, aided and later succeeded by Russell Clark. Aerodynamics were handled by Paul Baker and William Schoolfield with propulsion under James Shoemaker and his assistant, Don Jordan. Beisel himself dealt with design integration—making an airplane out of the various components—and deciding which concepts or changes to accept.

Sleek, clean, innovative: the Corsair was loaded with power and potential. Vought ranked with Lockheed and Northrop as an innovative manufacturer, and the promise was delivered when, on 1 October 1940, the prototype made 404 MPH (343 knots) in a straight line between Stratford and Hartford, Connecticut. In doing so, the Corsair probably became the first U.S. production aircraft capable of the then-magic 400 MPH mark in level flight, possibly excepting Lockheed's twin-engine XP-38 Lightning.

The author is grateful to the following photographers and collectors who generously devoted their time, talents, and collections to this volume. Frederick A. Johnsen (Attaboy First Class with Oak Leaf Cluster), Peter M. Bowers, and Dave Menard. Photos from the San Diego Aerospace Museum are identified as SDAM.

BARRETT TILLMAN
1996

*Dedicated to the memory of Boone T. Guyton—F4U test pilot and fellow Tailhooker.*

*F4U-1s of the original production batch with flat "birdcage" canopies prior to the hump for cockpit-mounted rear-view mirror. These Corsairs bear standard 1942 Navy color scheme of blue-gray upper surfaces and medium gray undersides with six-position stars: both sides of the fuselage and top as well as bottom of both wings.*

# DESIGNING **1** FOR SPEED

Vought's design team approached the F4U project with a philosophy of minimum drag and maximum thrust. That meant the cleanest, smallest possible fuselage behind the most powerful engine available. The all-metal monocoque airframe was as aerodynamically efficient as Vought engineers could manage: state of the art production techniques included spot welding and flush riveting. In fact, Vought and the Naval Aircraft Factory in Philadelphia had jointly perfected the spot-welding technique. The airscoops and intakes common to other high-performance aircraft of the era were notably absent from the Corsair's fuselage.

Instead, oil coolers for the engine were placed in the wingroots, where they incurred relatively less drag. Unlike some late 1930s fighters (notably the Spitfire and Me-109), the F4U's main landing gear was completely faired in when raised, and the tailwheel was also retractable.

Certainly the Vought fighter's most distinctive feature was its inverted gull wing, which had a symbiotic relationship to the engine. Pratt & Whitney's superb Double Wasp was an 18-cylinder aircooled radial displacing 2,804 cubic inches. The experimental XR-2800-4 version was employed in the prototype, with a two-stage supercharger and two-speed auxiliary blower. Originally, maximum rated power on takeoff was 1,805 horsepower—the most then available to any production fighter in the world. Republic's P-47 Thunderbolt, built at nearby Long Island, used the same engine.

### THE AWESOME DOUBLE WASP

The Double Wasp got its name from the engine's configuration:

*The prototype Corsair, XF4U-1 BuNo 1443, aloft over Hartford, Connecticut, in 1940. Noteworthy features are the original forward-set cockpit and armament of twin .50 cal. guns in the nose with one .30 cal. in each wing. The aircraft was bare aluminum overall except for chrome yellow wings on top and leading edge, with national emblems top and bottom of both wings.*

Called "the dive test airplane," the 17th production Corsair (BuNo 02169) was modified with prominent blisters to hold cameras aimed at the horizontal stabilizers during a series of progressively steeper and faster dives during late 1942. Precise dive and recovery profiles were flown by Vought test pilots, providing engineers with empirical data for comparison with sliderule calculations. High-G pullouts were an important part of factory testing, as the Corsair was among early production aircraft to encounter compressibility.

Close-up view of the starboard camera "blister" for recording the stress incurred during prolonged dive tests. Of note is the fact that the aft portion of the teardrop-shaped container has been fixed over the standard inspection panel beneath the rudder. Also, white "pasties" cover the other access panels, possibly to indicate whether they flexed sufficiently to become misaligned during high-G pullouts.

two banks of nine cylinders each, based upon previous P&W designs such as the R-2180 and the dead-end R-2600 dating from 1936. The R-2800 entered production in 1940, becoming the firm's first engine to exceed 100 horsepower per cylinder. Throughout the series, the R-2800 featured a 5.75-inch bore and 6-inch stroke.

The company devoted considerable engineering and test effort to perfecting metallurgy and cooling fins for the cylinders. The crankcase was an aluminum forging, the cylinder heads being forged. Late-production versions tipped the scales at a hefty 2,560 pounds, which still meant nearly one horsepower per pound.

Reliability of the Double Wasp was incredible. In one combat episode over the Philippines in late

## SECTION I

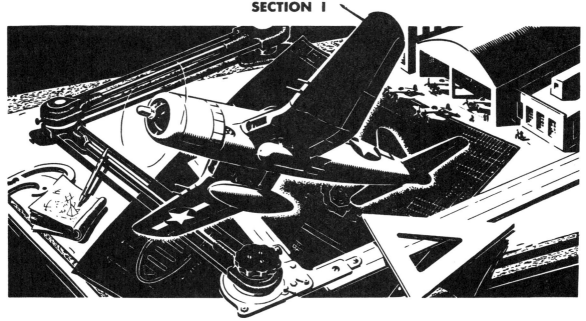

## DESCRIPTION, DIMENSIONS AND LEADING PARTICULARS

### 1. DESCRIPTION.

The *Corsair* is a single-place, single-engined, low-wing monoplane. Designed as a land- or carrier-based fighter by Chance Vought Aircraft Corporation, it is manufactured by Chance Vought Aircraft Corporation, Stratford, Connecticut, as the model F4U-1; by Brewster Aeronautical Corporation, Long Island City, New York, as the model F3A-1; and by Goodyear Aircraft Company, Akron, Ohio, as the model FG-1.

Structurally, the *Corsair* is designed chiefly about the center wing-fuselage section which supports the engine section, the fuselage, the main landing gear and the outer wing panels. In construction, the fuselage is of the semi-monocoque type, and the wing is a full cantilever type with a main spar and box beams. The airplane is fabricated mainly of metal; the outer wing panels are fabric-covered metal frames, the movable control surfaces being of either wooden or fabric-covered metal construction.

A Pratt and Whitney R-2800-8 or 8W Double Wasp air-cooled engine powers the *Corsair*. The engine has a two-stage supercharger and a water-injection system, and drives a three-bladed, constant-speed, hydromatic Hamilton propeller.

Hydraulically - powered wing - folding mechanisms, alighting and arresting gear, landing gear and wheel brakes are provided. The main landing gear retracts completely into the wing, and the tail wheel and arresting gear retract partially into the fuselage.

Distinguished characteristics of the *Corsair* are the long fuselage and the inverted gull wing.

### 2. PRINCIPAL DIMENSIONS.

Dimensions are given with the airplane in the level-flight position unless otherwise stated.

*a.* GENERAL. *(See figure 4.)*
Span (Wing spread) . . . . . . . . . . . . 40 ft. 11.726 in.
Span (Wing completely folded) . . . . . . 17 ft. .50 in.
Length (Over-all) . . . . . . . . . . . . . . . 33 ft. 4.688 in.
Height (Level-flight position
with struts extended) . . . . . . . . . . 15 ft. 3.775 in.
Height (Tip of propeller at top,
three point position) . . . . . . . . . . . . 15 ft. 0.79 in.
Height (Outer wing panels in
vertical position) . . . . . . . . . . . . . . . 18 ft. 3.2 in.
Height (Outer wing panels
completely folded) . . . . . . . . . . . 16 ft. 6 ± ½ in.

*b.* WINGS.
Center Section (Curve identi-
fication at root) . . . . . . . . . . . . . . . . NACA 23018
Outer Panel (Curve identi-
fication at root) . . . . . . . . . . . . . . . . NACA 23015

*Aesthetic pen-and-ink drawing from an F4U Erection and Maintenance manual ("Dash-2") shows a Corsair laden with an asymmetrical load of one bomb and one range-extending drop tank under its wings. The availability of more than one hard point allowed for stores configurations like this. (Bill Compton via Don Keller)*

*The same dive test aircraft (from the previous page) almost a year later, probably late 1943 or early 1944. The teardrop fairing on the vertical stabilizer has replaced the fuselage-mounted bulge but also seems positioned to permit photography of the grid squares on the fabric "flipper" surfaces to evaluate control response and stress in various high-G flight regimes.*

1944, a Hellcat pilot took a flak hit which punctured the engine case. He flew toward the water, streaming smoke "until the oil was all gone—then it quit smoking and we proceeded to the ship."

Certainly the Double Wasp was versatile. It powered five wartime Navy aircraft besides the Corsair (including the F6F through F8F plus Lockheed PV series and the Martin PBM Mariner) and several Army types such as the Republic P-47 Thunderbolt, Northrop P-61 Black Widow, and Curtiss C-46 Commando transport. Generally, Navy-procured engines were given even dash numbers while Army Air Forces orders had odd numbers: the R-2800-8 in the F4U/FG/F3A-1 series and the -51 in the C-46, for instance.

Pratt & Whitney's headquarters remained at East Hartford, Connecticut, but the company also opened a plant in Kansas City, Missouri. The R-2800 also was produced by three automotive subcontractors: Ford, Nash, and Chevrolet.

In the words of one industry authority, "the R-2800 started out as a very good engine and ended up as arguably the finest piston engine ever."

### That Cranked Wing

In order to benefit from the 2800's available power, Vought determined that a 13-foot, 4-inch diameter, three-blade propeller was necessary. A Hamilton Standard prop was selected, and little difficulty was met in mating it to the engine. However, the big "Ham Stand's" ground clearance was insufficient for conventional landing gear, so Beisel's crew decided to "crank" the wing, using the inverted gull design. Otherwise, with a low- or midlevel straight wing, the F4U would sacrifice some of its exceptional speed with too small a prop.

*Corsair exploded view from the Erection and Maintenance manual shows major assemblies that came together to make the F4U. As depicted, the F4U had a pair of aileron balance tabs (No. 19) on the wings, but an aileron trim tab only on the left side. (Bill Compton via Don Keller)*

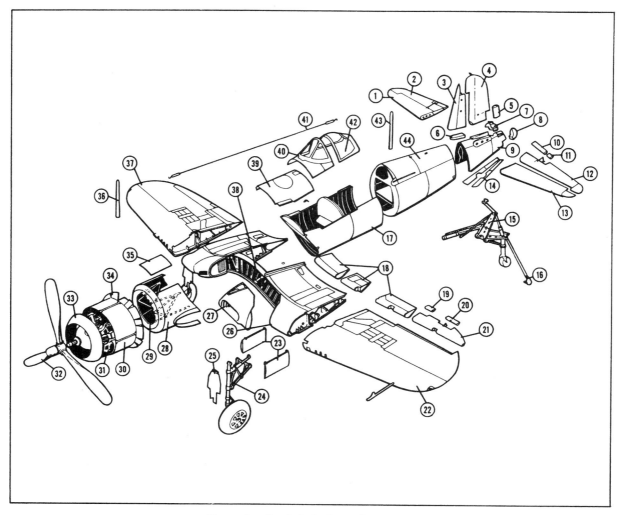

*Figure 3 — Exploded View of Corsair*

| | | | | | | |
|---|---|---|---|---|---|---|
| 1 | VS-34103 | Stabilizer—R.H. | 22 | VS-10013 | Outer Panel—L.H. |
| 2 | VS-33109 | Elevator—R.H. | 23 | VS-13593 | Doors Installation—Landing Gear |
| 3 | VS-10105 | Fin Assembly | 24 | VS-10275 | Landing Gear Assembly |
| 4 | VS-33107 | Rudder Assembly | 25 | VS-10857 | Fairing Installation |
| 5 | VS-10174 | Tab Assembly—Rudder | 26 | VS-34070 | Interbeam Assembly |
| 6 | VS-1522 | Fairing Installation | 27 | VS-37750 | Vane Assembly |
| 7 | VS-13128 | Fairing Installation | 28 | VS-10650 | Accessory Compartment Cowling |
| 8 | VS-19504 | Cone Assembly | 29 | VS-23602 | Engine Mount |
| 9 | VS-10229 | Aft Section | 30 | VS-10646 | Panel Assembly |
| 10 | VS-12148 | Trim Tab Assembly—Elevator | 31 | PW-R-2800-8W | Engine |
| 11 | VS-13114 | Balance Tab Assembly—Elevator | 32 | E6643A-21 | Propeller |
| 12 | VS-33109 | Elevator Assembly | 33 | VS-10620 | Nose Cowl |
| 13 | VS-34103 | Stabilizer Assembly—L.H. | 34 | VS-24655 | Flap Installation |
| 14 | VS-34282 | Front Door Assembly | 35 | VS-33329 | Panel Assembly |
| | VS-34293 | Rear Door Assembly | 36 | VS-33582 | Mast Assembly |
| 15 | VS-34226 | Tail Wheel Installation | 37 | VS-10013 | Outer Panel—R.H. |
| 16 | VS-11900 | Arresting Hook | 38 | VS-34072 | Main Beam Assembly—Center Section |
| 17 | VS-10225 | Front Section | 39 | VS-11835 | Cowl Assembly |
| 18 | VS-10069 | Flap Assembly— Center Section Inboard | 40 | VS-23815 | Windshield and Cowl Installation |
| | VS-10068 | Flap Assembly—Center Section Outboard | 41 | VS-10581 | Antenna Installation—Fixed |
| | VS-10067 | Flap Assembly—Outer Panel | 42 | VS-37849 | Sliding Section |
| 19 | VS-24013 | Balance Tab—Aileron | 43 | VS-17504 | Mast Assembly |
| 20 | VS-19830 | Trim Tab—Aileron | 44 | VS-33228 | Mid-Section Assembly |
| 21 | VS-24009 | Aileron Assembly | | | |

As with everything aeronautical, there were tradeoffs. Building the inverted gull wing was a demanding, costly process which tended to limit production potential for a peacetime aircraft. The up side of the equation was twofold: it permitted a shorter, lighter landing gear (and thus use of the full-size prop), and it added even more knots to the aircraft's top speed.

Wind tunnel tests demonstrated that a mid-wing position incurred less drag than a wing placed more toward the top or bottom of the fuselage. Vought's gull wing permitted a right-angle junction of the fuselage wing stub—in effect, a mid-wing attachment, with its attendant speed advantage. Additionally, systems which otherwise might have protruded from the fuselage (incurring additional drag penalty) were placed in the "bent" portion of the wing: oil coolers, intercoolers, and supercharger intakes.

The wing center section was of fairly conventional construction: an aluminum multi-part box spar involving the main spar and inter-spar, plus leading and trailing edges. The wing itself was based on a design from the National Advisory Council on Aeronautics: an NACA 2300 series airfoil with chord (width) ranging from 18% of span at the roots to half that value at the tips. Curve identification of the wing at the center section was NACA 23018; the outer panel at the same position being NACA 23015. Spanning 41 feet, the production Corsair's cranked wings were hydraulically folded over the canopy for maintenance or storage, reducing airframe width to just 17 feet.

The rest of the airframe was attached to the center section in three major segments. The forward fuselage, excepting the engine and accessory section, held the main fuel tank in production F4U-1s. (An additional 63 gallons were contained in each of the outer wing panels for a total 363 gallons of internal fuel.)

Attached immediately aft of the center section was the middle fuselage (almost nine feet in length) with several operational items: radio and navigation electronics; anchoring brackets for part of the arresting gear; elevator controls;

*Cockpit shot of BuNo 02169 showing instrumentation to monitor dive performance. The gunsight receptacle has been covered with a plexiglass cover in the center of the panel. Immediately to the left is the conventional "accelerometer" (G meter) reading up to 7 positive and one negative. The box to the right of the clear panel is a G meter specially installed for dive tests, with limits pegged at 12 positive and more than four negative. The horizontal panel below the G meters controls specially-installed tail cameras, with a nonstandard instrument showing propeller accumulator pressure.*

and rear cockpit items including fittings for the pilot's seat.

Finally, the empennage section (just under seven feet long) mounted the vertical and horizontal stabilizers, tailwheel mounts, and tailwheel gear doors. Sitting on its wheels, minus the engine, a production-line F4U-1 measured a little over 23 feet.

Dimensions of the F4U-1/FG-1/F3A-1 were listed by the Navy as follows:

Wing span (spread)  40 ft. 11.726 in.

Wing span (folded)  17 ft. 0.500 in.

Length overall  33 ft. 4.688 in.

Height (level flight, wheels down)  15 ft. 3.775 in.

Height (prop at top, 3-point position)  15 ft. 0.790 in.

Height (wings folded vertically)  18 ft. 3.200 in.

Height (wings completely folded)  16 ft. 6.000 in.

## THE PRODUCTION WAR

The Corsair first flew in May 1940, at the time Germany over-ran France. There followed the Battle of Britain, and of course by the end of 1941 the United States itself was fully engaged in the war. Consequently, BuAer and Vought were constantly concerned with upgrading the F4U in light of current combat experience.

Toward that end, Vought began a series of modifications to the basic design which would continue for 13 years. First, the R-2800 was upgraded to the -8 version, with 200 more horsepower which raised total output to 2,000. Plans also were undertaken to enhance what Russ Clark called "producibility," with production adapted to modular assembly. Airframe components

*Vought's final assembly line in December 1942, when the Navy accepted 68 F4U-1s. Completed aircraft roll down the line on the right while newly completed fuselage center sections (including wing stubs) await their turn on the left. Subcomponents are being produced in the next bay to the left, from where they will join the assembly line and emerge as completed aircraft in a matter of days. Vought delivered 178 fighters to the Navy and Marine Corps from July through December that year, but increased tenfold during 1943.*

*One photo is worth an accident report. This dash one probably fell victim to the early Corsair's potentially treacherous landing characteristics, circa late 1942. The crumpled port wing impacted the ground before the rest of the airframe, wheeling the fighter off the runway where it nosed up in soft dirt. The crash crew has taken over, as "Maryann," the generically-named crane, arrives to help lower the tail. (SDAM)*

thereby were manufactured more rapidly, leading to increased deliveries. Expensive, time-consuming prewar sub-assemblies which had been machined now were largely manufactured by forgings and extrusions.

As a large, sophisticated aircraft in its day, the Corsair was maintenance-intensive. The hydraulics were particularly complex for the landing gear and wing fold mechanisms, and the factory installed almost 100 inspection or access panels in the airframe; nearly 30 in each wing.

In order to enhance survivability, several changes were made on production F4U-1s, beginning with the unprotected wing center section fuel tanks, which were removed. A rubberized, self-sealing tank of 237 gallons was placed ahead of the cockpit, and the pilot's seat was moved 32 inches farther aft.

Pilot protection was enhanced with addition of 155 pounds of armor plate and a thick pane of bullet-resistant glass behind the windscreen. The flat "birdcage" canopy was made capable of being jettisoned in event of an emergency.

*Dimensioned three-view Corsair drawing from the Erection and Maintenance manual shows phenomena of the F4U's wing-folding mechanism: The Corsair achieved a maximum vertical height of just under 18 feet momentarily during the wing folding/unfolding cycle as wings reached vertical; at rest when folded, the wings only extended about 16 feet, 3 inches into the air. These dimensions could be critical for below-deck stowage; British Corsairs had clipped wingtips to accommodate lower vertical clearances aboard ship. Wings also hinged at an angle that caused the leading edge to appear to protrude forward as the wing folded, as called out with the line marked "L.E. Wing" in the drawing, instead of folding perpendicular to the thrust line (T.L. in the drawing). This forward angle increased as the wings achieved their completely folded position. (Compton/Keller)*

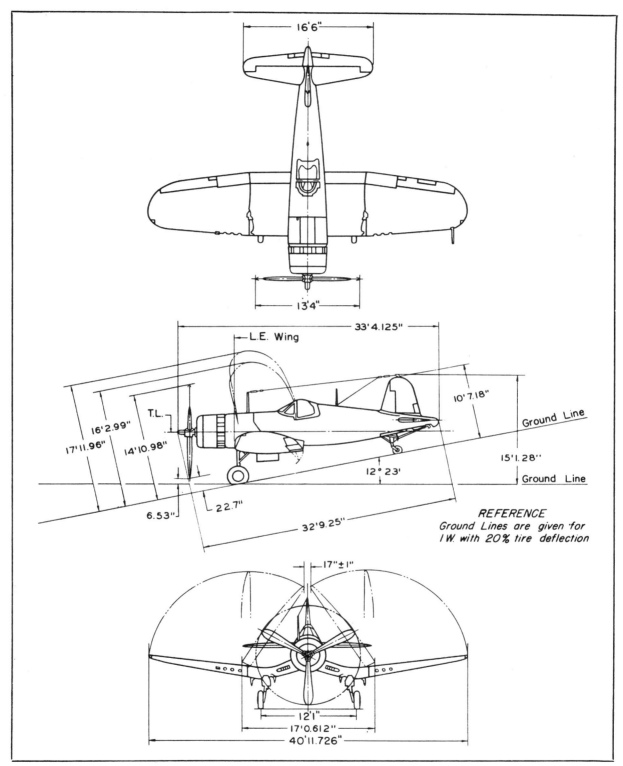

**Figure 4 — Principal Dimensions of Corsair**

*Vought Design No. 354 was this "one-off" two-seat F4U-1, built as an experimental transition trainer. Perhaps more than any other naval aircraft of WW II, the Corsair required careful handling by novice aviators, particularly in landing early dash ones before various fixes such as the wing leading-edge spoiler and modified landing gear. However, incorporation of such mods to production aircraft sufficiently tamed the F4U so that the two-seater was judged unnecessary.*

Armament was an early change in the Corsair. The prewar philosophy of mixed .30 and .50 caliber guns was abandoned in favor of six .50s, three in each wing, with a notable increase in ammunition. The fanciful concept of dropping ten light bombs onto enemy aircraft was also abandoned, and eventually Corsairs sprouted heavy bomb shackles and rocket rails.

Moving the guns to the wings increased .50 caliber capacity to 2,350 rounds—50 fewer than the F6F-3/5 Hellcat. The disparity was caused by the outboard gun in each wing, which lacked room for a full-length belt of linked ammo due to the inverted gull wing.

Low-speed handling characteristics were enhanced by changing the landing flap design and increasing the span of the ailerons. Boone Guyton had logged many hours in the prototype, experimenting with different control designs, and his work paid off handsomely.

Reflecting the increasing importance of radio and radar in aerial combat, the Navy installed identification, friend or foe (IFF) equipment.

Meanwhile, with the Pacific War in full swing, the fleet's Peter was constantly robbing Vought's Paul. Almost daily, three-foot-long teletypes arrived at Stratford listing the innumerable spare parts needed by growing Navy and Marine squadrons. Some 150 production or field retrofits were implemented, and their variety was endless: brake master cylinders, cowl flap and engine leaks, high-altitude ignition problems, plus what Clark termed "scores of nuisance items."

*An interesting contrast is evident in this early-production F4U-1 sporting late-war stars and bars with unusual individual aircraft markings. The squadron and location are unknown, but the small islet and auxiliary vessel indicate a rear area base, probably during early to mid 1944. (Mrs. David Perry, via SDAM)*

Finally, in November 1942,

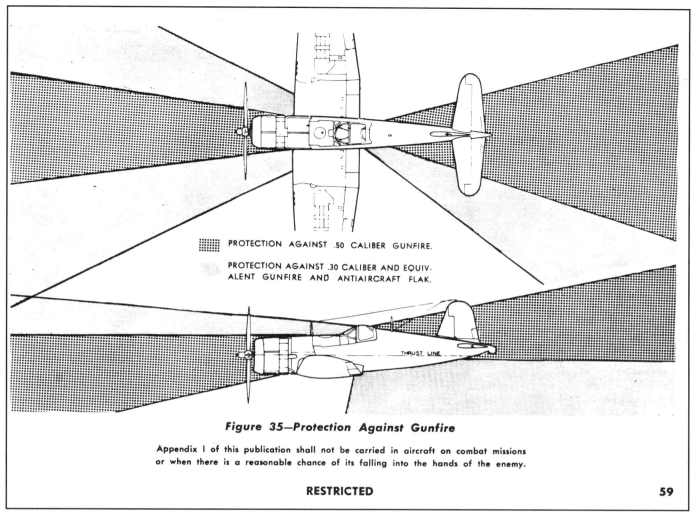

PROTECTION AGAINST .50 CALIBER GUNFIRE.

PROTECTION AGAINST .30 CALIBER AND EQUIV-
ALENT GUNFIRE AND ANTIAIRCRAFT FLAK.

THRUST LINE

*Figure 35—Protection Against Gunfire*

Appendix I of this publication shall not be carried in aircraft on combat missions
or when there is a reasonable chance of its falling into the hands of the enemy.

**RESTRICTED**                                                                    **59**

*Armor protection zones are shown for a late-model Corsair in this view from a "Dash-1" Flight Manual, showing
areas protected against .50-caliber and .30-caliber gunfire. Ruggedness contributed to the Corsair reputation.*

a month after Fighting Squadron 12 took delivery of its first Corsairs, the factory established a modification shop at NAS North Island, San Diego. There, Marine Air Base Group Two could modify squadron aircraft as needed without tapping the hard-pressed production line in Connecticut.

### Flight Testing the Corsair

Vought's F4U flight-test section started small and generally remained that way. Recalled Boone Guyton, "Bob Stanley and Bud Kelly departed (the flight test team) about the initiation of the XF4U-1 tests, leaving Lyman Bullard, chief of flight test, and myself. We then added pilots for both experimental and production tests as best we could from about 1942 on."

However, with America suddenly at war, experienced aviators in the civilian world were scarce commodities. Guyton remembered that from 1943 to 1946 the company operated with about six pilots in experimental flight test and 15 to 17 flying full-time in the production shop. "We obtained them as best possible," he said, noting that only Bullard and himself had been naval aviators.

The production test pilots— those who flew factory-fresh aircraft to ensure they were ready for Navy acceptance trials—came from varied backgrounds. There were flying instructors, crop dusters, fixed-base operators, and several "young engineer or close to engineer types who got some Cub time."

Guyton and a handful of the old pros raised the fledgling test pilots almost from the ground up. The aspirants were put through OS2U Kingfishers and SB2U Vindicators to get the feel of fleet type aircraft.

And then they were on their own

*The same aircraft (see page 14) showing long-term effects of exposure to the relentless Pacific environment. Modelers may take note of the hasty touchup paint applied to the vertical stabilizer and rudder, while the usual demarcation line between blue-gray upper and light gray undersurfaces has bleached somewhat as a result of prolonged sunlight. (Mrs. David Perry, via SDAM)*

*A classic head-on view of an early production F4U-1, showing the inverted gull wing to advantage. This photo well illustrates the aerodynamic benefits inherent to the distinctive configuration; compare the frontal "dish area" of the Corsair to the larger, oval-shaped cowlings of the F6F Hellcat and P-47 Thunderbolt, both of which used the same Pratt & Whitney R-2800 engine. By moving the oil coolers to the wingroots, Vought engineers minimized drag and gained approximately 35 knots in an airframe weighing about the same as the Grumman. F4U-1 (8,980 lbs empty) 417 MPH/20,000 ft; F6F-3 (9,100 lbs empty) 375 MPH/17,000 ft. (Peter M. Bowers)*

**WARBIRDTECH**
S E R I E S

in a six-ton airplane with 2,000 horsepower in their left hand and a huge nose that blocked out the world ahead. One of the production test pilots was Wolfgang Langewiesche, not only a superior aviator but a superior writer as well. Aside from the Corsair's exotic good looks, he was enthralled by its awesome speed: a limiting Mach number of .73 in a steep dive. By comparison, today modern airliners typically cruise that fast in level flight.

"You were in a new world," he recalled in 1977, "and saw things that only a few years earlier had been unknown. For instance, the vapor sheet: with a little extra speed, a little bit downhill, you pulled on the stick for a bit of extra G and a nice white sheet of cloud appeared on the top of the wing—atmospheric moisture condensing as the air was thinned out by the wing. You could make it come and go by pulling and relaxing on the stick."

As Bullard, Guyton, and other test pilots had discovered, the Corsair soon butted up against the invesible fence called compressibility. The preliminary "Mach tuck" in which a highspeed aircraft wanted to nose over past the vertical was a new phenomenom in the early 1940s. Langewiesche explained, "In the warm air of the Connecticut summer, you could reach the middle 500s (MPH) at around 10,000 feet, but it took an amazingly steep dive to reach a speed that is today's slow cruise."

One of the ironies of the Corsair test program was the requirement to continue "proof of contract" flights well after the F4U had entered combat. This seeming anomaly was driven by the fact that

The Corsair in its element near Stratford, Connecticut. The Navy's first order in June 1941 specified 584 aircraft—a figure that grew to more than 12,500 over the next 13 years. From the "dash one" to the AU-1 and F4U-7, the Corsair underwent 981 major engineering changes and perhaps 20,000 minor ones while becoming the most numerous carrier aircraft of all time. From an operational perspective, the most important modifications involved the landing gear, tail hook, and wing spoiler which "tamed" the F4U in the critical regime of carrier landings. (Peter M. Bowers)

the Corsair was needed far faster than even accelerated wartime efforts permitted. Thus, Goodyear test pilot Don Armstrong found himself performing routine tests in FG-1s to assure the Navy that the

Akron-built Corsairs met service standards even while Marine Corps pilots were bombing and strafing Japanese bases while flying identical aircraft.

An F4U-1 during Army Air Force evaluation at Wright Field, Dayton, Ohio, in 1942. Compared to existing USAAF fighters in squadron service, the Corsair was a spectacular performer. It was both faster and outclimbed the P-38F, P-39D, and P-40E, and had comparable top speed with the emerging P-47C while easily outclimbing the Thunderbolt. North American's P-51 series did not enter American service until that summer, but compared to the Royal Air Force's Allison-powered Mustang I, the Corsair was 35 MPH faster and climbed about 700 feet per minute better. (Peter M. Bowers)

# "CURING" THE CORSAIR

In the F4U-1, the U.S. Navy possessed a world-class fighter with more speed, power, and potential than anything else afloat. However, as a carrier aircraft it left much to be desired. In fact, Captain Eric Brown, the Royal Navy's vastly-experienced test pilot and world-record tailhooker, described the dash one U-bird as "a dog to deck land."

There were multiple problems, beginning with poor visibility from the cockpit. The low canopy restricted the pilot's view over the long nose (he sat 14 feet behind the propeller), which interfered with a satisfactory carrier approach. Visibility was further reduced by frequent hydraulic leaks from the multiple cowl flaps, resulting in streaking fluid on the windscreen. Leaky engine rocker boxes only compounded the problem. A production-line change was effected, with the upper cowl flaps being deleted and that portion of the fuselage permanently faired over.

Even in a perfect approach with a well-timed "cut" from the landing signal officer, the Corsair remained a handful. The stall characteristics, with a chilling left wing drop, required constant pilot attention and considerable skill in timing the impact with the deck.

Upon contacting the deck, nearly every landing resulted in full shock absorber compression, which in

*Though not identified in the official caption, this division of early F4U-1s almost certainly is from VF-12 at San Diego, the first fleet Corsair squadron. The Navy release of May 26, 1943 states, "These sleek, speedy, carrier-based planes are Vought CORSAIRS, the U.S. Navy's newest fighter plane. In Pacific actions in the last few months, they have scored spectacular success against Japanese Zero's (sic), outfighting the enemy plane in every action." In truth, Corsairs saw no carrier action until 1944, and occasionally came out on the short end during early combats in the Solomons. However, by war's end the F4U claimed an 11 to 1 kill-loss ration in aerial combat. (Tailhook)*

*Fresh from the factory to you: Vought employees crate a dash one Corsair for shipping. Gear retracted, the fuselage sits on the bottom of the palette as sides of the crate are moved into position. The propeller and outer wing panels also will be inserted before the crate is sealed and sent on its way to a fleet aircraft pool. (Warren D. Shipp via SDAM)*

*NAAS Los Alamitos, California, was a busy place. Aside from operational units undergoing training, routine air station maintenance also was performed. These sailors are changing an R-2800 engine on an F4U-1—no easy chore when the Wasp Major weighed about a ton "dry." Note the Interstate TDR-1 drone in the background. (SDAM)*

turn caused a serious bounce. Some landing attempts were spectacularly ineffective: during initial qualifications aboard USS *Charger* (CVE-30), one VF-17 pilot bounced as high as the masthead, crammed on power, and flew back to the beach without bothering to raise gear, hook, or flaps!

Fighting 17's engineering officer, Lt(jg) Merle Davenport, worked on the problem with Vought tech reps led by Jack Hospers. They tried varying combinations of oil level and air pressure within the landing gear struts and finally hit upon the right combination. With more air pressure in the strut, there was less impact on the oleos at touchdown, and therefore less tendency to bounce. It was a relatively "quick fix," easily duplicated on new aircraft arriving in the squadron.

Aside from bottoming out the landing gear oleos, another phenomenon was "hook skip"—the tailhook bouncing over the wires. In the days of straight-deck aircraft carriers, there were only two types of landings: "traps" and major accidents. The former was normal and earnestly desired, in which the aircraft's tailhook snagged a cross-deck wire and was "trapped" in the arresting gear.

The latter occurred when the plane missed the wires or bounced over the barriers into airplanes parked forward.

Eventually Navy engineers determined that many Corsair tailhooks were too light for the impact forces of a 60-knot touchdown on the flight deck. Consequently, even a good landing could turn to hash when the hook bounced off the deck, over the wire, and failed to arrest the aircraft's forward motion. The problem was solved by modifying the tailhook dashpot so that it further dampened out the recoil impulse and remained more or less level with the height of the arresting wires.

*"Blown canopy" F4U-1s roll down the production line, probably in early 1944. The aircraft are partly painted (wings and tail surfaces) but at this stage of construction are closely inspected for full assembly. An inspector's chalked notation on the vertical stabilizer says, "Tail on O.K." During 1944 the parent company produced 2,655 Corsairs while Goodyear delivered 2,108 and Brewster 599 for a total of 5,372, or an average of nearly 450 per month.*

*A transition period photo of an F4U-1 bearing 1943 tricolor paint scheme with late 1943 national insignia: "stars and bars" outlined by a narrow red border placed in four positions: fuselage sides plus upper left and lower right wings. This Corsair may have been a factory "holdback" for evaluation, as close examination reveals "F4U-1A" models parked in the background. Note absence of the tailhook and tail cone.*

*This F4U-1 was photographed in flight over MCAS Mojave, California, in January 1944. The late-version national insignia and nonstandard side numbers indicate that it was a "holdover" aircraft, one of eight Corsairs assigned to Headquarters Squadron of Marine Base Air Group 44. The "HedRon" also possessed 26 F4F or FM Wildcats, three SBDs, and an R5O transport. (SDAM)*

Carrier Replacement Air Group 12 at Alameda was one of two West Coast RAGs, and the fighter squadron began inauspiciously enough. On 15 October 1942 Lt. Cdr. Joseph Clifton's VF-12 had a lone F4F-4 on strength. The following month the air group moved to NAS San Diego, where it lost the RAG function and prepared for a combat deployment. On the first anniversary of Pearl Harbor, VF-12 boasted 15 new F4U-1s, becoming the Navy's original Corsair squadron. At the same time, nearby VMF-124 got the Marines' first F4Us.

By mid-January 1943, Clifton's "Peg Leg Petes" had absorbed 27 F4Us and Major William E. Gise's leathernecks were en route to the Pacific. The latter would introduce the Corsair to combat from Guadalcanal on 14 February.

Meanwhile, Air Group 17 had stood up at Norfolk, Virginia, and VF-17 became the third Corsair squadron with delivery of 13 Voughts by early March. Lt. Cdr. Tom Blackburn's crew immediately took to the piratical name of its aircraft and dubbed the squadron the "Jolly Rogers."

The rapid acquisition of so advanced an aircraft ensured there would be casualties. VF-12 lost seven Corsair pilots in training, though four of those perished in a single weather-related tragedy. In late July, owing to insufficient F4U spare parts, Joe Clifton's squadron converted to F6F-3s. VF-17 lost four aviators before deploying to combat, but none directly attributable to faults of the Corsair.

Both squadrons fought a continuing battle to get the F4U safely aboard ship, and solved the problems independently. Blackburn's VF-17 experienced a maddening series

*A tricolor painted F4U-1 of VF-17 aboard USS* Bunker Hill *(CV-17) during her shakedown cruise off Trinidad in July 1943. Beginning with* Essex *(CV-9), most ships of that class originally deployed with air groups matched to the ship's hull number. 17-Fox-8 displays full Stateside markings, which would be deleted in combat, though the squadron's pirate flag on the cowling became the trademark of the "Jolly Rogers." This Corsair has the bulged cockpit canopy with an integral rear-view mirror.*

*Fighting 17's new F4U-1s ride* Bunker Hill *through the Panama Canal in the summer of 1943. Distinctive in their tri-color schemes with "blown" cockpit canopies, these Corsairs were subsequently identified as F4U-1As—a designation which does not appear in most wartime sources. Lieutenant Commander Tom Blackburn's Jolly Rogers were bounced off their ship upon arrival in Hawaii owing to a lack of spare parts in the carrier pipeline and subsequently entered combat as a land-based squadron in the Solomons that fall.*

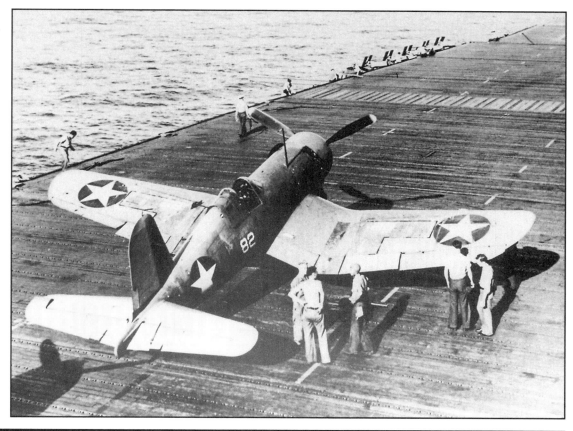

*A rare U-bird was this F4U-1 briefly assigned to USS* Enterprise *(CV-6) for carrier evaluation in late 1942 and early 1943. Generally flown by Lieutenant Stanley Vejtasa, the Corsair impressed the "Grumman-grown" fighter pilots, but the early dash ones required the finesse of a Swede Vejtasa to operate with routine safety in the demanding carrier environment. (Jim Sullivan via SDAM)*

Two for the price of one. FG-1 BuNos 13523 and 13566 had a taxi accident at Los Alamitos in May 1944, resulting in no little debris and a great deal of engine oil on the tarmac. The engine nose case with attached propeller of one participant rests beneath the nose of its "partner" in the episode—dramatic proof of the potential for disaster inherent in the Corsair's long nose. (SDAM)

"I said it was a good day, not a great day." FG-1D of VMF-512 is off-loaded from USS Gilbert Islands (CVE-107) following an "incident" on 11 March 1945. The squadron was part of Marine Carrier Air Group Two under Lieutenant Colonel W.R. Campbell, which subsequently participated in the Okinawa campaign and supported the allied landings at Balikpapan. (M.L. Stanton coll. via Tailhook)

of incidents aboard USS *Bunker Hill* (CV-17) during her summer 1943 shakedown off Trinidad. Despite apparently normal landings, several Corsairs failed to engage the arresting wires, bounced over the barriers, and in Blackburn's words, "strewing expensive debris in all directions, often as not breaking in two at the engine mount."

Despite the vexatious scrutiny of aviators and engineers, the problem was detected by an observant sailor of *Bunker Hill's* arresting-gear crew. He noticed a number of furrows in the new pine planks of the flight deck, running lengthwise from the stern. The problem had been absent from the squadron's initial carrier qualifications aboard the CVE *Charger*.

Examination of some crashed Corsairs revealed that the tailhook tips had sheared off—a fact overlooked in the greater excitement of untangling a six-ton airplane from its brethren parked forward of the barriers. Because the Naval Aircraft Factory had designed the hook points in the shape of an ax blade, they tended to dig into *Bunker Hill's* uncured wood, whereas little *Charger's* deck was older and therefore tougher. Consequently, if a pilot missed his wire, the hook plowed a trough up the deck until it sheared on a steel crossdeck drain channel.

NAF quickly redesigned the hook point, and the problem was solved. In connection with the modified landing gear oleos and homegrown wing spoilers to tame the Corsair's vicious stall, the hook fix helped make a civilized carrier aircraft of the F4U.

Blackburn's Fighting 17 inaugurated the Corsair to combat in November 1943, at the same time as Lt.Cdr. Gus Widhelm's night fighter outfit, VF(N)-75. By then, Clifton's VF-12 was also blooded, but had exchanged Corsairs for Hellcats before boarding *Saratoga* (CV-3) in August.

August was also the month that the F4U became dominant among Marine Corps fighter squadrons. The F4F Wildcat, though somewhat long in the tooth, still had claws and remained a front-line fighter until late summer. But the Corsair lineup in the Navy and Marines showed 26 squadrons, including 11 in the Pacific:

*Among the more distinctive markings of WW II Marine squadrons was the vertical rectangle of VMF-122, superimposed on gloss blue F4U-1Ds. The side numbers probably represent the last three digit of each aircraft's Bureau of Aeronautics number—a standard practice in Leatherneck squadrons from 1943 onward. During its first combat tour, November 1942-July 1943 the squadron was credited with 48.5 shootdowns in the Solomons, mainly in Wildcats. The second tour, under three COs, was devoted wholly to ground support and strikes in the Palaus from October 1944 on. (SDAM)*

VMF-114 was assigned to Marine Air Group 11, supporting ground troops in the Palau Islands where it earned a Navy Unit Citation in 1944-45. This FG-1D carries an external loadout of fuel tank and napalm canister for a close air support mission. Though 114 had no chance at aerial combat, the squadron counted three aces among its COs: Maj. Edmund F. Overend (a former Flying Tiger), Capt. Robert F. Stout (KIA), and Maj. Herbert "Trigger" Long. This photo has erroneously appeared with a caption placing the venue at Kadena Airfield, Okinawa.

Among the ten Marine squadrons assigned to Navy air groups were VMF-216 and 217 aboard USS Wasp (CV-18) in February and March 1945. This F4U-1D has recovered after a mission on February 12, en route to strikes against Japan. The two Leatherneck squadrons claimed four aerial victories during their abbreviated cruise. In order to accommodate the Corsairs, Air Group 81 "beached" its SB2Cs and reduced TBMs to 15 Avengers. Wasp's resident Hellcat squadron, VF-81, claimed 43 kills between November 1944 and March 1945.

BuNo 02522 (Above), the 370th production Corsair with other first batch F4U-1s under civilian guard at the Vought factory in 1942. This excellent shot of the tailwheel assembly and arresting hook gives an indication of troubles yet to come. The first two Navy squadrons with F4Us, VF-12 and VF-17, experienced serious difficulty in making safe carrier landings. Eventually the problem was traced to hook tips which tended to break on engagement with the flight deck as well as inadequate dash pots that permitted "hook skip" over the arresting wires. Both problems were solved by the autumn of 1943. (Peter M. Bowers)

A few Corsairs were employed as test beds during the war, as was this modified-canopy dash one in 1944. The cylindrical object beneath the fuselage was an experimental ramjet engine affixed to the F4U airframe for flight evaluation. The location is thought to be NAS Anacostia in the District of Columbia, site of much Navy flight testing before opening of the dedicated test facility at Patuxent River, Maryland. (Peter M. Bowers)

| | | | | | |
|---|---|---|---|---|---|
| VMF-211<br>En route SoPac | Maj. R.A. Harvey<br>33 F4U-1s | VMF-221<br>Russells | Maj. M.K. Payton<br>19 F4U-1s | VMF-321<br>Oak Grove | Maj. G.H. Knott<br>15 F4U-1s |
| VMF-212<br>Midway | Maj. S.B. O'Neill, Jr.<br>22 F4U-1s | VMF-223<br>El Toro | Maj. M.E. Carl<br>15 F4U-1s | VMF-322<br>Oak Grove | Maj. F.M. Rauschenbach<br>18 F4U-1s |
| VMF-213<br>Guadalcanal | Maj. G.J. Weissenberger<br>19 F4U-1s | VMF-224<br>En route SoPac | Maj. D.D. Irwin<br>18 F4U-1s | VMF-323<br>Cherry Point | Maj. G.C. Axtell, Jr.<br>9 F4U-1s |
| VMF-214<br>Russells | Maj. J.R. Burnett<br>19 F4U-1s | VMF-225<br>Mojave | Capt. J.R. Amende, Jr.<br>6 F4U-1s | VMO-351<br>Cherry Point | Maj. R.B. Cox<br>2 F4U-1s |
| VMF-215<br>Guadalcanal | Capt. J.L. Neefus<br>19 F4U-1s | VMF-311<br>Parris Island | Maj. J.D. Kane<br>18 F4U-1s | VMF-422<br>Santa Barbara | Maj. J.S. MacLaughlin<br>13 F4U-1s |
| VMF-216<br>El Centro | Maj. R.J. Morrell, Jr.<br>18 F4U-1s, FG-1s | VMF-312<br>Parris Island | Maj. R.M. Day<br>10 F4U-1s | VMF(N)-532<br>Cherry Point | Maj. E.V. Vaughn<br>8 F4U-2s |

*"I said it was a good landing, not a great landing." This F4U-1A missed the arresting wires and came to grief during a landing attempt aboard an escort carrier. The unusual checkerboard nose and tail are unknown to any combat units, and it is suspected that No. 50 may belong to Marine Air Base Group Two, which employed similar markings late in the war. (SDAM)*

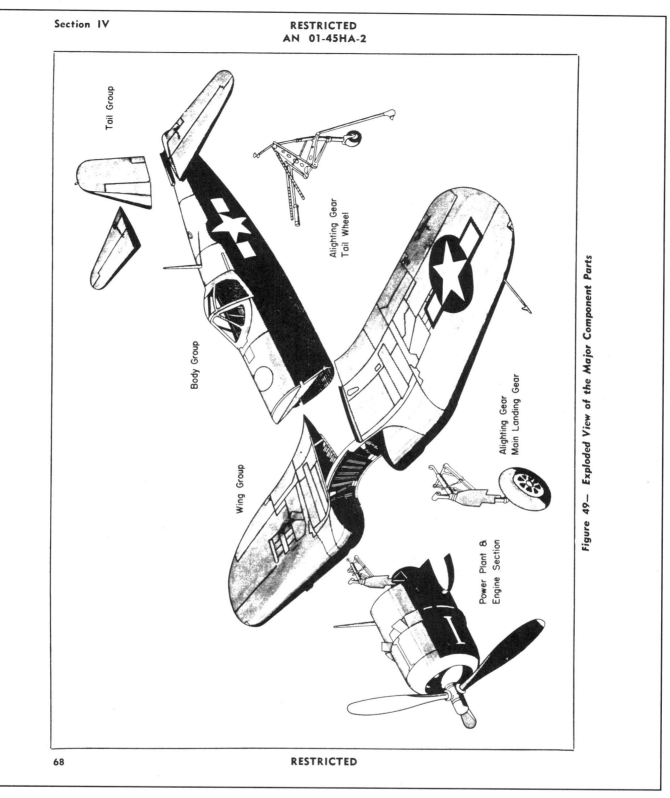

Tail Group

Alighting Gear
Tail Wheel

Body Group

Wing Group

Alighting Gear
Main Landing Gear

Power Plant &
Engine Section

*Figure 49— Exploded View of the Major Component Parts*

*Major component drawing from a Corsair Erection and Maintenance manual dissects the F4U into ungainly, unwieldy-looking sections that metamorphosed into one of the most strikingly aesthetic fighters of any era when assembled. Powerplant section mated to the rest of the fuselage at a canted station ahead of the gas tank. Drawing depicts cowl flaps open except at the top of the fuselage. This was in response to early problems with a top cowl flap section causing hydraulic fluid and oil to blow back on the pilot's windscreen. (Compton/Keller)*

# ARMAMENT

**M**achine guns, cannon, bombs, and rockets all were part of the F4U's armory. However, by a huge margin the most common battery was six Browning-designed Colt M2 aircraft machine guns, firing .50 caliber ammunition from disintegrating link belts.

The three guns in each wing were installed "in echelon" to allow feed chutes to reach the breeches. The inboard gun was farthest forward, with the outboard receiver farthest aft. Four guns were provided with two 200-round ammunition boxes, the exception being the aft outboard box which, in order to fit the wing contour, was shallower and held 175 rounds. Thus, the Corsair's total ammo capacity was 2,350 rounds.

Ordinarily the six Brownings were boresighted to converge their pattern of fire at 1,000 feet ahead of the aircraft. Squadrons varied, depending upon their mission priorities, but typically the zone covered by the pattern was a circular area from three to six feet in diameter. A one-second burst from six .50 calibers delivered 80 rounds within that circle.

The three most common .50 caliber ammunition types were ball, tracer, and armor-piercing incendiary. They were belted in various combinations, again depending upon squadron preference and mission requirements. For instance, some units or individual pilots disliked tracers because they warned an otherwise unwary enemy aviator that he was under attack. If the first burst missed—a frequent occurrence—the sudden light show flashing around the target aircraft removed all doubt as to its peril. Other fighter pilots liked tracers as an aiming aid, while some squadrons used them as the last several rounds in each gun to indicate an impending status of "ammo minus."

Fifty caliber ball was nearly identical to most rifle bullets: a lead core with a copper jacket. In the potent M2 round, it provided substantial penetration on soft targets such as aluminum aircraft structures or unarmored vehicles.

Armor-piercing incendiaries (APIs) were dual-purpose ammunition. With a steel penetrator core beneath the copper jacket, they contained a small amount of phosphorous which could ignite when shot through armor plate into fuel tanks.

None of these types had exactly the same ballistic characteristics.

*Wearing tropical pith helmets, a Marine ordnance crew hoists a Corsair with block and tackle at a South Pacific base. Once in level flight position, the F4U's six .50 caliber machine guns will be boresighted—aligned with a fixed target which duplicates the desired point of impact, usually 1,000 feet ahead of the aircraft. (SDAM)*

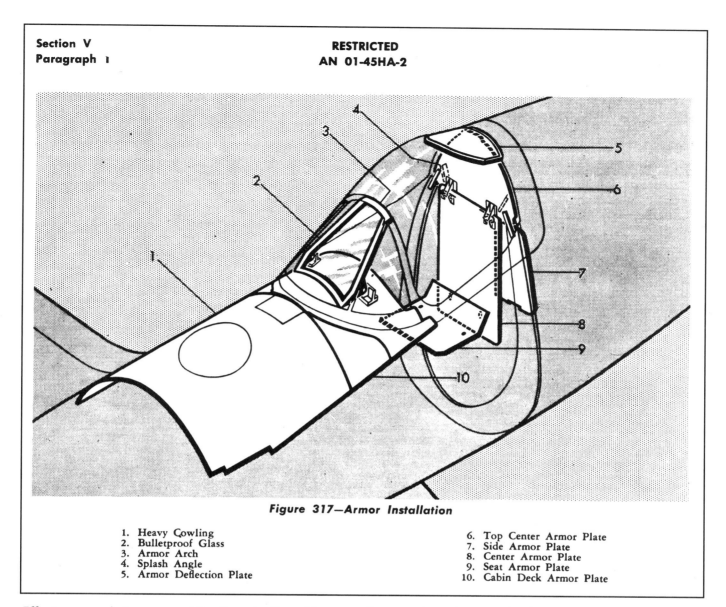

**Figure 317—Armor Installation**

1. Heavy Cowling
2. Bulletproof Glass
3. Armor Arch
4. Splash Angle
5. Armor Deflection Plate

6. Top Center Armor Plate
7. Side Armor Plate
8. Center Armor Plate
9. Seat Armor Plate
10. Cabin Deck Armor Plate

*Effort was made to surround the Corsair pilot with armor. Part number 1 is upper fuselage armor to protect the gas tank; the characteristic hooded look of Corsair canopies was provided by an armor deflection plate (part number 5) protecting the pilot from attacks above and behind the aircraft. It is easy to visualize a twisting dogfight in which an enemy would try for a deflection shot that coulde enter the canopy as the Corsair was in a tight turn, making this upper surface armor valuable. More armor protected the back and bottom of the pilot's seat. (Bill Compton via Don Keller)*

Ball bullets typically weighed 709 grains, or about 1.6 ounces. The other types usually weighed more, and consequently followed somewhat different flight paths over the preferred 333 yards to the target. However, considering the dense pattern fired from six heavy machine guns, and the flight time of less than half a second, the discrepancies were minimized.

The F4U-1C appeared in 1944, sporting four 20mm cannon in place of six .50 calibers. The "dash one Charlie" carried 924 rounds, which was increased to 984 in the F4U-4B of the Korean War era.

Pilots had individual preferences regarding armament. It is probably safe to say that most advocated the .50s, which not only carried two and a half times more ammo, but gave a far denser pattern at the target. However, some aviators preferred the greater penetration and explosive capacity of the 20 millimeters, even with less ammunition and a slower rate of fire.

*F4U-1D BuNo 57569 assigned to NAS Patuxent River's armament test (hence the AT-12 code) division. The new Corsair packs an awesome loadout of two Tiny Tim 11.75-inch rockets on the hardpoints, plus five-inch high-velocity aerial rockets (HVARs) on the "zero-length" rails beneath the wings. Though Tiny Tim packed a tremendous punch, it proved erratic and unreliable and was seldom used in combat. No. 569's naval career lasted less than a year: accepted in August 1944, it served in "Arm Test" until January and was stricken at Mustin Field in July 1945.*

*Air Group 84 Corsairs fully armed with eight HVARs beneath their folded wings aboard USS Bunker Hill (CV-17) in April 1945. With three F4U squadrons (VF-84, VMF-221 and -451), "CAG-84" was one of the most potent of the fast carrier air groups at the time of the Okinawa invasion on April Fool's Day 1945. However, CV-17 sustained severe kamikaze damage on 11 May, ending her combat career with heavy loss of life. (SDAM)*

During much of World War Two, and virtually all of Korea, the Corsair functioned as a fighter bomber. Consequently, its repertoire of air-to-ground ordnance expanded considerably. In the F4U-1D/FG-1D and F4U-4 variants, underwing bomb pylons and rocket rails were the means for delivering the equivalent of as much or more weight of power as a destroyer's broadside from five-inch guns.

In some instances, Corsairs took off with 3,000-pound bomb loads, but two 500-pounders or a single half-ton weapon was far more common.

External fuel tanks or special-purpose napalm bombs also could be carried on the pylons. The jellied gasoline, named for its combination of napthetic and palmitic acids, exploded on impact and spread a fiery oval across the target area to a distance of as much as 250 feet. It was especially useful in exposing camouflaged emplacements by burning off the foliage or netting over the facility.

During World War Two, aerial rockets were widely used in a variety of configurations. Mounted on "zero length" rails beneath the F4U's outer wing panels, they generally came in two types: 3.5 and 5-inch warheads on either standard or high-velocity rounds. The latter were preferred, as HVARs (high-velocity aerial rockets) had longer range, a flatter trajectory, and greater penetrating potential against reinforced targets such as concrete bunkers. Individual aircraft's wiring could be different within a unit, but generally the pilot's stick grip trigger controlled the guns while the bombs and rockets were fired by a button atop

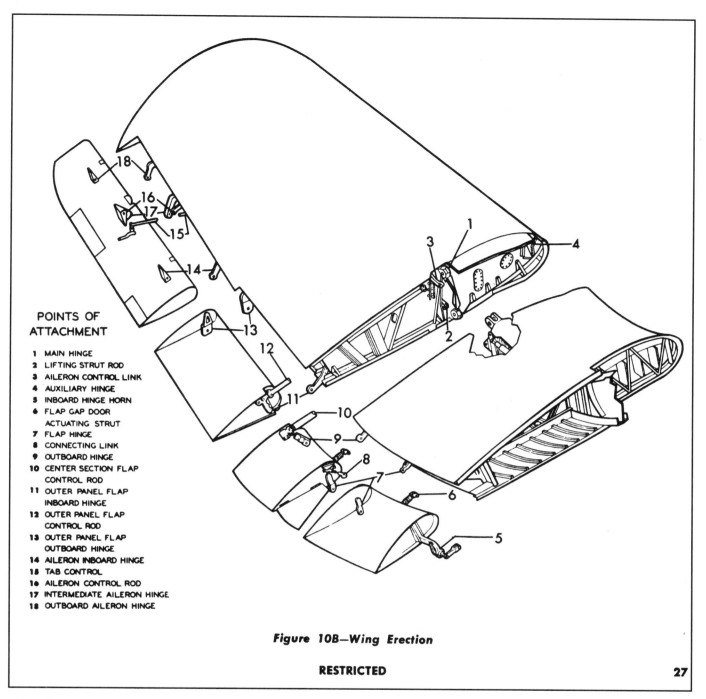

POINTS OF
ATTACHMENT

1 MAIN HINGE
2 LIFTING STRUT ROD
3 AILERON CONTROL LINK
4 AUXILIARY HINGE
5 INBOARD HINGE HORN
6 FLAP GAP DOOR
  ACTUATING STRUT
7 FLAP HINGE
8 CONNECTING LINK
9 OUTBOARD HINGE
10 CENTER SECTION FLAP
   CONTROL ROD
11 OUTER PANEL FLAP
   INBOARD HINGE
12 OUTER PANEL FLAP
   CONTROL ROD
13 OUTER PANEL FLAP
   OUTBOARD HINGE
14 AILERON INBOARD HINGE
15 TAB CONTROL
16 AILERON CONTROL ROD
17 INTERMEDIATE AILERON HINGE
18 OUTBOARD AILERON HINGE

Figure 10B—Wing Erection

27

*Wing flaps on the Corsair were segmented to accommodate the gull-winged trailing edge. Large ailerons were fabric-covered wooden structures. Placement of main wing fold hinge (part number 1) and auxiliary hinge (part number 4) well forward along the chord of the wing accounts for the angle the wings assume relative to the thrust line of the fuselage as they fold. (Compton/Keller)*

the stick. Which one was selected depended upon the position of the bomb-rocket transfer switch in the cockpit.

Land-based F4Us generally could take off with gross-weight ordnance loads, assuming a long enough runway. Carrier squadrons depended upon the amount of wind over the deck, even with a catapult-assisted launch. Consequently, during the Korean War most air groups devised standardized loadouts depending upon the mission requirement and amount of wind. "Load Able" might include full ammunition, a 1,000-pound

*A Vought formation shot of two F4U-1Ds which demonstrate the 1944 change in color scheme. The near aircraft, in tricolor pattern, carries a pair of 1,000-pound bombs on the underwing pylons. The far Corsair, possibly BuNo 57490, is gloss blue overall except for the flat-finish antiglare panel from the windscreen to the nose.*

*This beautiful shot of a mint-condition F4U-1A shows the type to advantage: flaps lowered, the leading-edge spoiler on the starboard wing which improved stall characteristics, and the bulged canopy which gave far better visibility. This view also shows the demarcation lines of the mid-war three-tone paint scheme, including sea-blue paint on the undersurfaces of the outer wing panels. The Navy decided that rather than painting them Insignia White to match the belly and wing stubs, the folding portion should be dark when viewed from overhead with wings stowed.*

bomb (or two 500s), and six rockets. "Load Baker" might include ammo, a 500-pounder, and four rockets. "Load Charlie" would be the lightest combination of ammunition and four or only two rockets.

### GUNSIGHTS

Throughout most of World War Two, Corsair pilots squinted through the standard Mark VIII reflector sight. Like most sights of its type, the Mark VIII projected an image, or sight reticle, onto a sloped glass via illumination from a light bulb housed within the base of the sight. The yellow-white reticle appeared superimposed on infinity, presenting the pilot with a center dot or pipper surrounded by two concentric rings.

The pipper was a mil dot: a spot of light which covered one foot of space at 1,000 feet distance—the range at which the fighter's six machine guns were set to converge. The inner circle about the dot measured 50 mils to the center, or 50 feet at 1,000 feet; the outer circle represented 100 mils to the center.

Given knowledge of the wingspan of enemy aircraft, it was possible to gauge when the target airplane was within firing range. For instance, a G4M Betty's 25-meter (82-foot) wingspan between the pipper and the 100-mil ring equalled 820 feet distance—slightly inside boresight range. Similarly, an A6M5 Zero had a wingspan of 11 meters, or 36 feet. To an F4U pilot dead astern of the Mitsubishi fighter, when the target's wingtips covered 50 mils, he was 720 feet away. In both cases the Corsair pilot knew that he could open fire with confidence of being well within effective range.

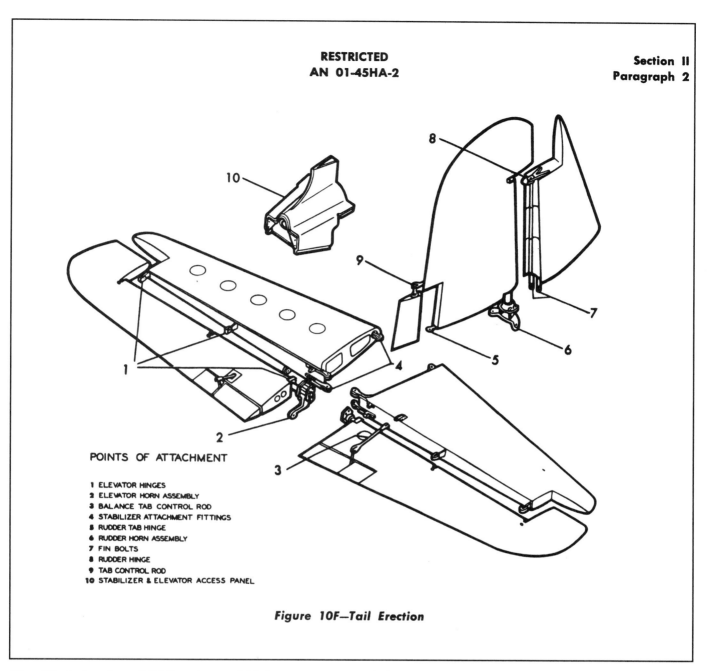

POINTS OF ATTACHMENT

1 ELEVATOR HINGES
2 ELEVATOR HORN ASSEMBLY
3 BALANCE TAB CONTROL ROD
4 STABILIZER ATTACHMENT FITTINGS
5 RUDDER TAB HINGE
6 RUDDER HORN ASSEMBLY
7 FIN BOLTS
8 RUDDER HINGE
9 TAB CONTROL ROD
10 STABILIZER & ELEVATOR ACCESS PANEL

**Figure 10F—Tail Erection**

*Simplified view from F4U Erection and Maintenance manual shows relationship of components of the tail group. Trim tabs are depicted on both elevators, no doubt of great use in dive recovery.*

However, dead astern shots were rare in aerial combat. More frequently, fighter pilots had to accept pot luck in the form of crossing shots which required them to "lead" the target: to shoot at a point in space ahead of the target's flight path so that the Zero and the .50 caliber bullets arrived at that point simultaneously.

The Mark VIII sight permitted high angle-off gunnery with some degree of confidence. The formula for wide deflection shooting was based on two constants: the speed of the target airplane and the speed of the bullets. The latter left the muzzle at about 2,800 feet per second, decelerating to an average of 2,500 foot-seconds; the former

could be estimated within broad parameters.

Since a .50 caliber bullet took $^4/_{10}$ of a second to travel 1,000 feet, it was possible to compute how much lead to allow in hitting, say, a twin-engine bomber. A Betty might cruise at 150 knots, or 175 MPH. Thus came into play the "two-thirds rule": the rough computation that at 90 degrees deflection and 1,000 feet range, the correct lead in mils was two-thirds the target speed in knots. Therefore, a 150-knot target required a 100-mil lead. A 200-knot target required 150 mils of lead: half again the distance from the 100-mil ring to the pipper, or three-quarters of the full diameter of the outer ring.

Deflection angles between zero and 90 degrees also were governed by a few rules of thumb. Full deflection values could be used from 90 to 60 degrees; three-quarters of full deflection from 60 to 30 degrees; half deflection from 30 to 15 degrees; and one-quarter or less thereafter. Again taking our hypothetical Betty bomber as the target, a quartering run at 30 degrees deflection would require only half the normal value lead: 50 instead of 100 mils in the sight.

Even cool-headed, experienced fighter pilots found it difficult to do the mathematical gymnastics required to calculate correct deflection in the few seconds available in combat. Consequently, the Mark VIII reticle provided a mental template as to how a target should appear within firing parameters. Through practice and repetition, it was possible to imprint the proper sight picture in an aviator's mind: "In this position, put the pipper here and *fire.*"

With 400 rounds per machine gun, the Corsair pilot had about 30 seconds of shooting time—assuming he used all six Brownings simultaneously. In some instances pilots "turned off" two guns in order to conserve ammunition, either as a means of engaging additional targets or, in the words of one ace, "to get me home." Given proper circumstances, a few F4U pilots employed their ammunition with disciplined economy, and nine became aces in a day—seven Marine and two Navy. Of these, the record was held by Ensign Alfred Lerch of VF-10 who, near Okinawa on 6 April 1945, shot down seven Japanese aircraft before returning to *Intrepid.* His division leader, Lt(jg) Philip Kirkwood, bagged six. A Marine pilot, Major Jefferson Dorroh of VMF-323, splashed six Val dive bombers in his only combat of the war on the 22nd of that month. Two other VMF-323 "Death Rattlers" bagged five apiece in the same combat.

### Gun Camera

A 16MM motion-picture camera was installed in the leading edge of the right outer wing panel, synchronized with the trigger. Ordinarily the model was an AN-N4A "gunsight aiming point camera" mounted behind a curved, laminated glass faired into the wing. By means of a boresight adapter, the camera could be arranged to focus on the convergence point ("harmonization") of the Corsair's guns—commonly 1,000 feet ahead of the aircraft. The camera bay had a self-contained heater to help ensure functioning in the frigid temperatures of medium to high altitudes. Additionally, the N-4 series cameras could be fitted with filters for the lenses, depending upon atmospheric conditions.

*Factory-fresh F4U-1D with underwing pylons visible. The hardpoints could accept either auxiliary fuel tanks or ordnance, which expanded the Corsair's versatility both for range and mission options. A peculiar aspect of this aircraft's armament is the thin transparent tape over the muzzle ports of the six .50-caliber machine guns. Generally, "100 MPH" duct tape was used, as it was more durable and gave greater protection to the Browning guns' barrels.*

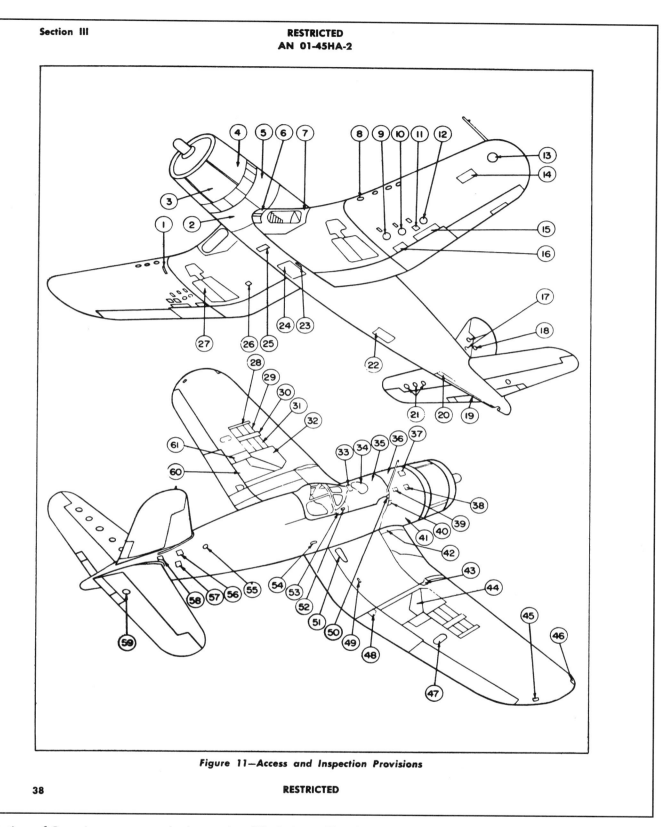

Figure 11—Access and Inspection Provisions

*Depiction of Corsair access panels shows simplified view of landing gear doors in the closed position. Main doors (part 27) consisted of two panels that hinged down to allow the gear to extend down and forward while twisting 90 degrees. Third door is mounted to main gear strut and serves secondary function as a dive brake. (Bill Compton/Don Keller)*

VOUGHT
# F4U CORSAIR

# The F4U-2

**T**wo Corsair models were devoted to the esoteric mission of night interception. Each was committed to that limited role in a specific theater of operations, against different enemies, a decade apart.

The first were 32 standard F4U-1s (most sources erroneously report 12) which probably should have been designated F4U-1Ns. Instead, they were called F4U-2s, which were committed to three squadrons—two Navy and one Marine. They employed hand-built radar sets designated XAIA: Experimental Airborne Intercept (Model) A.

Night Fighting Squadron 75 was established 1 April 1943 at NAS Quonset Point, Rhode Island. Under Commander William J. Widhelm, FitRon 75 had five other pilots and two nonflying officers. The squadron's six Corsairs were received between 1 and 25 June, allowing each pilot about 15 hours "in type" before departing Quonset Point on 2 August. Filled out with two radar officers, a dozen enlisted men, and an engineer from Sperry Gyroscope Company, Gus Widhelm's small command arrived at Espiritu Santo, New Hebrides, on 11 September. Combat operations

*Night fighting F4U-2s of VMF(N)-532 preparing to launch from USS* White Plains *(CVE-66) en route to their combat assignment on Tarawa Atoll in January 1944. During a nine-month tour Night Fighting 532 claimed two nocturnal victories while flying from bases throughout the Central Pacific. Another F4U-2 squadron, VF(N)-75, was land-based in the Solomons during 1943-44 while its offshoot, VF(N)-101, flew a split tour from* Enterprise *(CV-6) and* Intrepid *(CV-11) in the first half of 1944.*

*Major Everette Vaughan, skipper of VMF(N)-532, based on Roi in the Marshal Islands, early 1944. Most of the squadron's Corsairs had personal identities, and the CO's Number 201 was "Shirley June." Vaughan was the only 532 commanding officer during its combat deployment, finally relinquishing command in late September 1944. (SDAM)*

began from Munda Island, in the New Georgia Group, 12 nights later.

Between then and 31 January 1944, Fighting 75 logged 977 flight hours (163 per pilot) from Munda and, after 10 December, from Torokina airstrip on Bougainville. Six enemy aircraft were confirmed shot down under the direction of ground-control intercept (GCI) station "Moon."

Modifying the standard "dash one" Corsair for its nocturnal mission involved more than installing a radar set and hanging a scanner dish on one wing. The following secret report of 1 March 1944 details VF(N)-75's "mods" to the F4U-1:

The F4U as modified for night-fighting is designated F4U-2. Those modifications are:

WINGS

(1) The starboard wing panel is modified to support the scanner.

(2) The outboard starboard gun is removed to permit the installation of the wave-guide between the scanner and the junction.

FUSELAGE

(1) The arresting hook has been removed because, not being needed for land-based operations, its 9-lb. weight is saved (CG is thereby moved forward 1.8%).

ENGINE

(1) Exhaust flame dampeners are attached.

ARMAMENT

(1) See WINGS above.

(2) The remaining five .50s are a) boresighted to converse at 250 yards, instead of the normal pattern; b) pointed slightly upwards so that the F4U-2 can approach beneath the enemy's slipstream, and the point of convergence will be clearly visible above the cowling; c) belted with 250 rounds each, for interceptor and patrol work, instead of the normal 450 rounds (this is to compensate for the extra weight of the night fighter equipment); d)

loaded with alternate AP and Incendiaries (no tracers are loaded because their glare would impair the pilot's vision and they would disclose the plane's position).

COCKPIT

Major modifications:

(1) The radar control panel—containing the radar switch, the scanner selector, the operating switch and the tuning switch—is on the starboard side.

(2) The radio support panel, aft of the pilot, is completely filled with radar equipment.

(3) The radio equipment is beneath the pilot's seat.

Minor modifications:

(1) The A-B stage switch, with which the scope is changed from sweep (Stage A) to gunsight (Stage B), is directly outboard of the throttle, and can be released with the left thumb without removing the hand from the throttle.

(2) The instrument panel: a) the PPI scope is placed at the top center; b) the altitude instruments are on either side of the scope; c) the needle ball is below; d) the secondary instruments are grouped with navigation on the port side of the panel, and engine on the starboard;

e) dials are skeleton-numbered, with most of the intermediate numbers omitted.

(3) Lighting: a) indirect red, with perfect rheostat control; b) black felt anti-glare outer panel.

At present, conversion of the F4U to the F4U-2 is made only at NAF Philadelphia. The process consumes about 6 weeks and approximately doubles the cost of the plane. The change and redistribution of equipment penalizes speed by about 10 knots (2 knots for the flame dampers, 8 knots for the scanner); subtracts about 235 lbs from the total weight * and moves CG about 6% further aft. Most pilots

*VMF(N)-532's Number 212, apparently with the late 1943 national insignia encircled by a red border. The white radome seems to diminish the overall camouflage scheme, but some early radar housings were painted light colors to enable more thorough inspection of the sensitive units.*

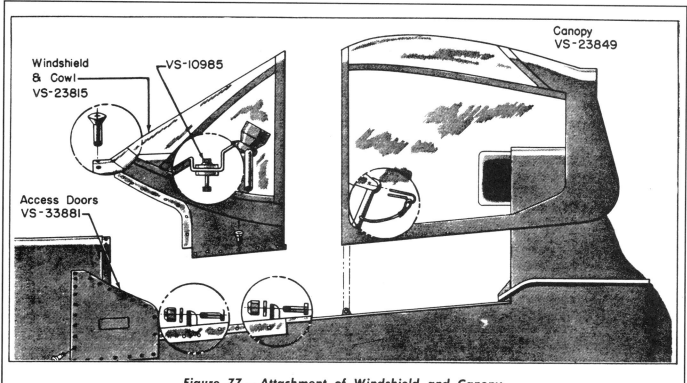

**Figure 77 — Attachment of Windshield and Canopy**

*The slight upward bulge of the Corsair canopy, introduced on the F4U-1A and subsequent models, allowed for higher mounting of the pilot's seat for better visibility over the long nose. The drawing depicts curved windscreen in use until a flat armored front windscreen was introduced during F4U-4 production. The older curved style could carry a partial armor glass panel mounted inside the cockpit.* (Compton/Keller)

agree that the handling characteristics are not appreciably affected.

**\* ADD:**

| | |
|---|---:|
| flame dampers (est.) | 8 |
| scanner, wave guide, cables, radar | 300 |
| **Total add** | **308.0** |

**LOSS:**

| | |
|---|---:|
| One .50 gun plus load of 450 rounds | 211.1 |
| 4 x 250 rounds removed from other guns | 322.5 |
| arresting hook (est.) | 9.0 |
| **Total loss** | **542.6** |
| **NET LOSS** | **234.6** |

### Airborne Radar Equipment

The F4U-2s of VF(N)-75 are equipped with the XAIA radar, built by the Sperry Gyroscope Co., Inc. XAIA is 3 centimeters in frequency and has an average power output of 40 watts. A dipole radiates the transmitted impulse and receives the return echo. The dipole is mounted on a scanner—a dish 18 inches in diameter—which is enclosed in a nacelle faired into the starboard wing, 3 feet from the tip. The scanner searches a cone whose apex is the scanner, whose axis is dead ahead, whose angle of rotation is 60 degrees, and whose altitude is 3 miles.

The scanner revolves at 1,200 RPM, completing its search every second and projecting it onto a screen on the instrument panel as a 3-dimensional picture. Azimuth is read from the target's position to the left or right of the scope's center line, which is an extension of the plane's longitudinal axis. Range is read from its position on the vertical scale, which is graduated from 3 miles at the top to 0 at the bottom. Relative altitude is read from the semaphore indicator. This is a pair of dots, the left one, known as "the reference dot," being the plane's indicator, and the one hardby to the right, the target indicator. Thus, if the right dot shows above the reference dot, the target is above the night fighter t the same angle as the angle between the two dots and at the distance shown on the vertical scale.

As the night fighter reduces the altitude differential, the imaginary line joining the two dots becomes more nearly horizontal; and as he closes range, the dots move down the vertical scale, toward 0 range. When, however, the range is indicated as ½ mile or less, the pilot shifts his instrument from Stage A (used for ranges between 3 miles and ½ mile) to Stage B, or "gunsight" (used for ranges less than ½ mile).

The transmitted impulse now moves in a circular path whose angle of rotation is 7 degrees instead of the former 60, and the echo's strength (and therefore the target's range) is indicated by the length of the "wings" which "grow" on both sides of the scope's vertical line. As long as the night fighter remains dead astern of the target, these wings are equally spaced on each side of the line. When they have grown enough to reach the "goal posts," the target is dead ahead at 250 yards, which is the focal range of the five guns, and the pilot fires.

In the present experience of VF(N)-75, the advantages of the radar gunsight are largely theoretical, since at no time have Japanese tactics been such as to warrant switching from Stage A to Stage B. Even if the equipment functioned perfectly, the radar gunsight would not be needed, since operational orders in most fields of action require positive visual identification of a target plane.

### FIRST KILL

For an aircraft designed as a carrier-based day fighter, the height of irony was attained when the Corsair's first combat occurred as a land-based night fighter.

The VF(N)-75 mission report is reprinted here verbatim:

DATE:
31 October 1943.

MISSION:
Night fighter interception.

TIME:
TTO 2130, Contact 2300, ATA 2340.

GCI:
Moon.

PLACE:
Vicinity of Shortland Islands.

FORCES ENGAGED
Own: 1 F4U-2, Lt. H.D. O'Neill, USN, VF(N)-75.

ENEMY:
1 Betty.

ALTITUDE OF CONTACTS:
10,000' and 7,500'

RESULTS:
Betty shot down in flames, confirmed.

NARRATIVE:
O'Neill was vectored onto the bogey and made visual contact 12 miles SE of Shortland. The Betty had no flame dampers, and exhausts were "bright as running lights and clearly visible from every position." The first contact was made with the a/c on opposite courses, Betty at 10,000' and O'Neill at 12,000'. Betty's evasive tactics were slow turns. O'Neill came down and fired his first burst from 150/250 yards. Betty's starboard engine burst into flames, but they died or were extinguished quickly. O'Neill turned and on his second pass - at 7,500' - fired from 150 yards from dead astern. Betty took fire and crashed into the water, being followed all the way down by Shortland lights.

O'Neill reports that his AIA worked exceptionally well. Much St. Elmo's Fire. Between 2230-2445, considerable 90mm AA from Shortland. O'Neill expended a total of only 128 rounds.

Less than nine hours later, Lt.Cdr. Tom Blackburn, skipper of VF-17, shot down two Zekes to begin the Corsair's daytime record.

The other F4U-2 squadrons were VF(N)-101, formed from Widhelm's cadre in January 1944, and VMF(N)-532, established in 1943. FitRon 101, under Lt.Cdr. Richard E. Harmer, deployed two detachments with the Fast Carrier Task Force, embarked in USS *Enterprise* (CV-6) and *Intrepid* (CV-11). Harmer's own "det" scored five kills before leaving "The Big E" in July 1944 while the "Evil I" Corsairs saw no significant action.

Maj. Everette Vaughan's 532 was established at MCAS Cherry Point, N.C., on 1 April 1943 and arrived at Tarawa Atoll in January 1944. While based in the Central Pacific the squadron shot down two enemy night fliers and returned to the West Coast in October 1944.

### THE HIGH-FLYING, SHORT-LIVED F4U-3

Six months before Pearl Harbor, the Navy had been interested in a study of the Corsair's high-altitude potential: upwards of 40,000 feet or more. Apparently the project languished until the summer of 1943, when Vought designer Russell Clark was called to a meeting at the Bureau of Aeronautics to discuss

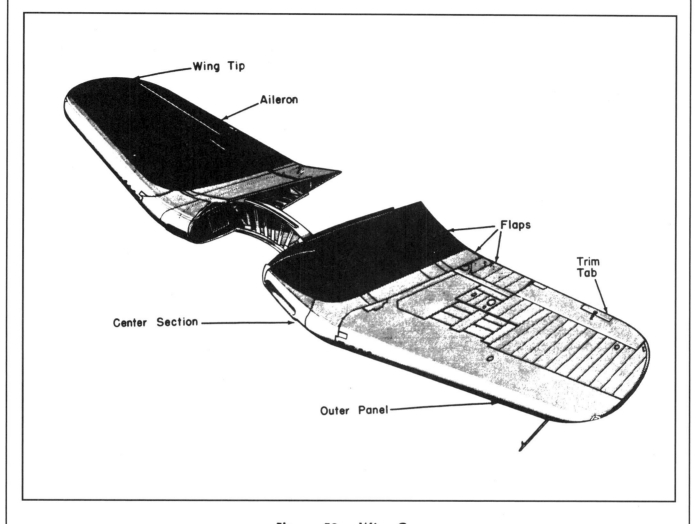

**Figure 50— Wing Group**

*A key to the strength of the Corsair was the built-up arched main wing beam, passing through the fuselage, as shown in the "Dash-2" F4U manual. Parallel lines extending to the wingtip in the drawing represent ribs in the area of the outer wing that was fabric covered on many production Corsairs up to F4U-5s.*

prospects for gaining additional altitude for the Corsair. At the heart of the proposal was an experimental Bierman supercharger produced by the Turbo-Engineering Company in New Jersey.

Navy engineers had investigated the possibility of installing two of the exhaust-driven turbo super-chargers in an F4U, one on each side of the engine. There appeared some promise for enhanced high altitude performance from the extra power provided by the Bierman designed supercharger.

Consequently, Vought modified three F4U-1s (designated XF4U-3A -3B and -3C) with an XR-2800-16 Series C engine mated to the 1009A supercharger. Almost simultaneously, 27 Goodyear aircraft (FG-3s) were also intended for upgrading against the possibility of full-scale production. The dash three Corsairs were identifiable by chin-mounted air scoops at the bottom of the engine cowling.

Actual flight tests began in April 1944, by which time the Goodyear batch had been cut to 13 aircraft. Initial results were encouraging, as tests demonstrated an output of 2,000 horsepower at 40,000 feet, and a reserve of power at 50,000 feet. "However," recalled Clark, "the superchargers were immature mechanically. Our mean time between failures was almost one flight (!) so we abandoned the program and had to wait for the F4U-4 to get to 'higher ground.'"

### F4U-4: The Pilot's Airplane

Some of the potential in the XF4U-3 was realized in the F4U-4, without most of the attendant problems. Seven prototypes (BuNos 49763, 50301, and 80759-763) were built to iron out the still challenging task of mating Pratt and Whitney's more powerful Series C Double Wasp to the bigger, beefier airframe.

Because pilots would be pulling more power from the R-2800-18W, the engine required redesign to higher performance than had previously been needed. Consequently, vital components such as cylinders were strengthened while improved cooling was engineered into the new powerplant. The "W" suffix on the model 18 engine, of course, referred to water-methanol injection which permitted higher combat power settings for limited periods. While the dash 18 engine was boosted to 2,100 horsepower, the "wet" option gave aviators an eye-watering 2,450 horsepower for up to about five minutes.

In order to make full use of the F4U-4's engine, a bigger four-blade propeller was installed to optimize the potential.

Five F4U-1s were taken off the line and modified to dash four prototypes, first flying in April 1944. A year later production aircraft were chasing *kamikazes* at Okinawa.

With the -18 engine came some engineering changes in the airframe. Carburetor inlets, originally mounted in the wingroots, were moved to the "lip" at the bottom of the cowling.

The first prototype, designated XF4U-4XA, was flown on 19 April 1944, with the second (XF4U-4XB) that July. The new U-Bird was clocked nearly 25 knots faster than the F4U-1 series, making 379 knots (446 MPH) at 26,200 feet.

Aside from increased power, the dash four absorbed much of the collective input from factory and military pilots regarding handling characteristics. Though the -1A series had offered improved carrier landing traits, the Corsair still was a demanding aircraft to get aboard. The new Corsair promised even better carrier landing traits.

Subsequent X-jobs featured a new cockpit layout and a one-piece canopy. The layout gave more thought to instrument grouping for pilots, and enhanced mechanic "user friendliness." For instance, the armored pilot's seat now was hinged to provide easier access to the radio. Vought first flew the semi-final version XF4U-4 on 7 October 1944, which the Navy accepted at month's end.

The dash four probably had more variants than any Corsair model. Early on, the Royal Navy version was given the designation F4U-4B, but the war ended before the Fleet Air Arm acquired any such aircraft.

Similarly, Goodyear was to have begun production of the equivalent FG-4.

Beginning in January 1945, F4U-4Cs were produced with four 20mm cannon as standard armament. The first of these 300 aircraft reached Okinawa with Marine Air Group 31. Launched from the escort carriers *Breton* (CVE-23) and *Sitkoh Bay* (CVE-86), they flew ashore on L-Day plus seven (7 April) in time to intercept inbound *kamikazes*.

Limited-production models were photo-recon F4U-4Ps and night fighting -4Es and -4Ns with APS-4 and APS-6 radars, respectively. With the -4C's cannon armament, they would have been potent adversaries in the night skies over Japan when Operation Downfall kicked off in November 1945.

The increase in speed and power was not gained without a penalty. Empty weight of the F4U-4 was 9,205 pounds, or a relatively modest 203-pound increase over the dash one—part of the increase being additional armor plate. Gross weight climbed to 14,670 pounds, with external stores accounting for most of the difference.

Dash four Corsairs were fighter-bombers in every sense of the word. Aside from pylons for two 1,000-pound bombs, they had four sets of zero-length rocket rails beneath each wing. The combination of a fast, rugged aircraft with a variety of weapons rendered the F4U-4 a powerful weapon in both World War Two and Korea—what Marine riflemen and GIs began calling "the sweetheart of Okinawa."

# BUILT FOR 5 COMFORT

## THE DASH FOUR AND FIVE

Following World War Two, the U.S. defense industry underwent significant changes. The most immediate, of course, were inevitable "downsizing" (to employ the 1990s term) which resulted in canceled contracts and reduction in the work force.

For Vought Aircraft, an even more drastic change was afoot. Concern over the vulnerability of much of America's industry to emerging missile technology led to relocating the factory from the maritime Northeast to Dallas, Texas. There the firm set about perfecting the Corsair for the postwar world—and the emerging cold war with the Soviet Union.

Thus was born the F4U-5.

With the R-2800-32W engine, or Twin Wasp Series E, the dash five was identifiable by the "cheek" inlets on the cowling (as opposed to the -4's "chin" inlet), which accommodated twin auxiliary blowers. Thus, Vought engineers redesigned the forward fuselage to accept the wider profile, and mounted the engine more than two degrees downward to enhance longitudinal stability. The new arrangement carried a bonus in that the pilot gained improved forward visibility as well.

The F4U-5 featured other innovations in the Corsair line. The outer wing panels were aluminum covered rather than fabric, giving the new U-bird additional streamlining and, therefore, more speed. In fact, the dash five was rated at more than 460 MPH, or an honest 400 knots in level flight.

Pilot comfort was raised to new levels in the latest fighter. Manual or automatically operated cowl flaps and supercharger were new

*F4U-5 BuNo 121800 of VF-13 after disastrous landing attempt at Jacksonville on 5 April 1950. The dash five, though perfected for pilot comfort and ease of operation, proved difficult to maintain and experienced a rash of engine problems. It was most identifiable by its "cheek" air intakes as opposed to the "chin" mounted intake on the F4U-4. (SDAM)*

features, and spring tabs on elevators and rudder could reduce pilot effort by nearly 40 percent. With a high-altitude mission in mind, the dash five also came "factory equipped" with electrically heated guns and pitot tube, and more efficient cockpit heating. With these features, the penultimate Corsair could operate at altitudes approaching 45,000 feet.

Vought rearranged some of the cockpit geometry, making more switches, dials, and controls more accessible. Recalled Boone Guyton, "With the F4U-4 we had eliminated most of the Corsair's handling problems. The 'five' was to upgrade the best traits of the F4U-4 and employ the latest technical advances commensurate with reciprocating engine fighters."

Guyton logged the first flight of the new U-Bird, BuNo 97364, on 7 September 1947. The "customer"— the Corsair pilot—was catered to as he never had been before. Automated controls were designed and installed for supercharger, cowling, and intercooler flaps as well as oil cooler doors.

Line of sight for the pilot, seat contour and reclining angle, seat to rudder pedal distance, plus innovations such as armrests and folding pedals all were aimed at easing pilot fatigue. Long-range missions over ocean expanses were envisioned as a norm for the new Corsair, and aviators generally gave their new mounts high marks for cockpit design and comfort. The first dash fives joined *Franklin D. Roosevelt's* (CVB-42) Air Group Three in early 1948.

However, the new Corsair had problems specific to the type. One of the more subtle—and most dangerous—was the gyro horizon, which differed from previous types. Though a non-tumbling gyro was installed, the wings were displayed below the artificial horizon when climbing and above the horizon when descending. Nobody from Vought or BuAer could account for the illogical presentation, which was blamed for two unnecessary deaths. A pair of ensigns in Air Group Two returning from a training mission in August 1948 were never seen again. Local weather involved lowering ceilings, and it was assumed that the young pilots had relied upon their unusual gyro horizons with fatal results. Thereafter, conventional gyro displays were installed.

*The XF4U-3B, BuNo 17516, second of an experimental batch of three high-altitude Corsairs which led to the F4U-4. The dash three was derived from the F4U-1 airframe and the XR-2800-16 (Series C) engine with a Bierman supercharger, hence the prominent airscoop under the cowling. Tests as high as 50,000 feet were conducted with the F4U-3s, but the requirement proved unnecessary.* (Fred Johnsen)

*F4U-5 BuNo 121982 of VF-13 crashed on Runway 23 at NAS Jacksonville, Florida, 20 May 1950. The ensign at the controls walked away with no more than a bruised ego. (SDAM)*

Other problems specific to the F4U-5 were harder to correct. Quipped one VF-42 pilot, "In order to start the thing in extremely cold weather, it was first necessary to catch it on fire about three times." The -32W engine became infamous for quirkiness, as illustrated by an example from NAS Norfolk, circa 1948.

The dash five's throttle system was controlled by oil pressure rather than by direct linkage, and a few days after the first planes arrived, plane captains made an unwelcome discovery. After starting the engines for a routine warmup, several aircraft developed serious power surges, causing the Corsairs to jump their chocks and collide with aircraft parked ahead of them.

*F4U-5 of Fighting 13 is craned onto a flatbed truck at Jacksonville, Florida, on 15 August 1950. After sustaining strike damage during embarked operations, T-310 was salvaged from St. John's. (SDAM)*

Close inspection revealed no apparent reason for the surge.

Then someone noticed that a cold front had passed the previous evening, causing the oil in the linkage to congeal while the throttle setting remained at its previous position, regardless of the plane captain's actions. Pratt & Whitney was duly notified, and redesigned the engine controls with a mechanical linkage. Other difficulties involved operating the engine at power settings as high as 75 inches of manifold pressure, and use of 145-octane gasoline.

Aside from technical glitches, the dash five also gave problems operationally. Though the F4U-4's hydraulically-operated tailhook had given little difficulty, the -5 reverted to the previous latch type, which slowed flight deck cycles. More importantly, the five-inch longer fuselage of the new Corsair resulted in nose heaviness which caused airframe damage in offcenter carrier landings. VF-23 had especially bad luck during *Coral Sea's* (CVB-43) shakedown cruise in 1948. The resultant warped fuselages and popped rivets reduced the squadron to only three flying aircraft in a few weeks.

In all, the F4U-5 made only six deployments with four air groups from 1949 to 1953. Two Marine Corps squadrons flew the type, including VMF-212 which went to Korea in 1950 but had to exchange them for dash fours.

The F4U-5 ended its service with Naval Reserve units in 1956.

### NIGHT STALKER: THE F4U-5N

Interim night fighters were F4U-4Ns with AN/APS-5 radar and -4Es with the more popular APS-4. However, none of the handful produced ever reached combat, and it is uncertain they were even assigned to squadrons.

The ultimate Corsair night fighters were 315 F4U-5Ns, including those modified for cold-weather operations in the -5NL variant. At the heart of the weapon system was the AN/APS-19 radar, capable of four operating modes: 150-mile navigation; 100-mile search and detection; 20-mile interception of

*During a carrier qualification period, F4U-5 BuNo 12182 of unlucky VF-13 noses up after missing USS* Wright's *(CVL-49) number six wire. Air Group One, with VF-13 and 14, made the last three of only six F4U-5 carrier deployments, riding* Coral Sea *(CVB-43),* Wasp *(CV-18) and* Franklin D. Roosevelt *(CVA-42) between 1951 and 1953. (SDAM)*

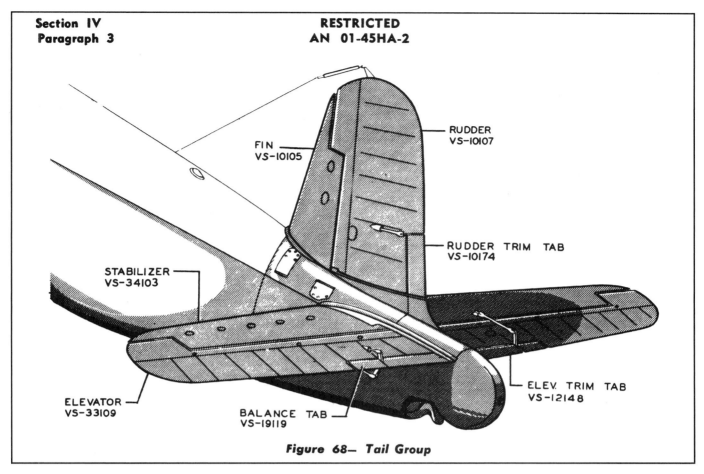

FIN
VS-10105

RUDDER
VS-10107

RUDDER TRIM TAB
VS-10174

STABILIZER
VS-34103

ELEV. TRIM TAB
VS-12148

ELEVATOR
VS-33109

BALANCE TAB
VS-19119

**Figure 68— Tail Group**

*The F4U Erection and Maintenance manual, in naval parlance, says: "Port and starboard stabilizers are identical and may be interchanged. They are connected to the fuselage at three main attachment points..." The vertical fin is mounted with a decided offset (not visible in this drawing) to cope with high torque. The business end of the tailhook is visible in a notch in the bottom of the fuselage; by F4U-5 production, the hook was completely enclosed and flush with the fuselage when retracted. (Bill Compton collection via Don Keller)*

airborne targets; and a blind-fire capability optimistically rated to 1,500 yards. However, as with the World War Two "dash two" night fighters, rules of engagement prohibited firing upon a bogey without positive visual identification.

A typical night fighter engagement began with the pilot turning his radar function control to "Intercept" with the range selector to the 20-mile grid. His scan angle switch was then set at the 130-degree setting (135 for the APS-19A upgrade) with the target aircraft about two-thirds of a mile ahead.

When the pilot saw the target echo on his screen, he switched the range control to the lowest which would accommodate the signal. In "Intercept" mode, the APS-19 operating ranges decreased from the initial 20-mile setting to eight and then to two nautical miles.

Closing the distance, the night fighter pilot maneuvered to place the target echo squarely in the center of his scope. He steered by reference to the two dots displayed in phosphors on his screen: elevation (height) and azimuth (bearing). Ideally, the midpoint of the two images was centered upon zero

azimuth, with the dots aligned horizontally.

Pressing within visual range of the bogey, the Corsair pilot continued in "Intercept" mode until within two-thirds of a mile (1,500 yards). He could gauge that relative distance by the echo's placement on the scope: roughly one-third up from the scope's lower edge while using the two-mile range function.

At this point the night fighter probably was nearing visual range. Assuming it was hostile, and the controller had cleared him to fire, the pilot switched to "Aim" mode.

F4U-5 BuNo 121837, Ensign D. Mealy driving, loses its port mainmount aboard USS Oriskany (CV-34) on 17 January 1951. The wheel, with tire attached, bounces over the aft elevator while the four-blade prop narrowly misses shaving "O Boat's" teak flight deck. (SDAM)

F4U-5 BuNo 121985 aboard FDR, at the start of the last dash five deployment on 1 June 1953. Lieutenant B.J. Lunsford suffered a collapsed starboard landing gear oleo, apparently after an ordnance flight, as an unexpended rocket remains on one of the port rails. (SDAM)

He continued his approach on a collision course until the horizontal trace covered most of the radar screen. If the trace represented less than the full screen, the pilot knew that his target was not straight ahead, and would have to acquire the bogey visually for final approach.

The pilot, having armed his guns, then switched his scan to the illuminated gunsight and presumably pressed the trigger. At that point his six .50 calibers or four 20mms completed the job.

During the Korean War, Marine Corps F4U-5Ns flew with VMF(N)-513. Operating from advanced airfields in South Korea, the nocturnal Corsairs claimed two kills during 1951-52, a record matched by -513's F7F-3N Tigercats. The second of the Corsair kills, on 7 June 1952, made an ace of Lt. John Andre, who had logged four victories as an F6F night fighter pilot in World War Two.

However, the most successful American night fighter of the war was the jet-powered Douglas F3D-2 Skyknight, which gained seven kills in Marine service and four more with the Navy.

Navy F4U-5Ns and -5NLs participated in virtually every big-deck (Essex-class) carrier deployment of the war, from June 1950 to July 1953. Ordinarily the VFN detachment consisted of four aircraft either from the dedicated Pacific Fleet night fighter squadron, Composite Squadron Three (VC-3), or its Atlantic Fleet counterpart, VC-4. However, no carrier-based aerial victories were claimed by Corsair night fighters. By far their most valuable contribution was nocturnal interdiction and strike missions against Chinese and North Korean supply routes.

*F4U-5NLs of VC-4, the Navy's Atlantic Fleet night fighter squadron, circa 1953. Composite Squadron Four sent four- or five-plane detachments to deploying carriers, providing all-weather interception capability to LantFleet air groups, primarily in the Mediterranean Sea. However, by the end of the Korean War the squadron also had Douglas F3D-3 Skyknight jets, with one detachment from USS Lake Champlain (CVA-39) logging combat missions.*

Near the end of the war, in June 1953, the VC-3 Team Dog from USS *Princeton* (CVA-37) went ashore to deal with enemy night-flying "Bedcheck Charlies." Lt. Guy Bordelon's det was "op-conned" to Fifth Air Force, operating under USAF control in an effort to prevent the slow, low-flying Communist aircraft from harassing U.S. and allied troops. Air Force F-94 jets had proven unable to accomplish the mission, and thus the Corsairs were sent in. During three intercepts between 29 June and 17, Bordelon claimed five Yaks or LaGGs shot down, becoming the only Navy ace of the war.

## WINTERIZING THE -5N

Korea's freezing climate was an ally to the Communist ground forces, who were experienced in cold-weather operations. Naturally, with winter came worse flying weather, which further aided Chinese and North Korean troops who had long since ceded air supremacy to the allied powers.

In order to enhance F4U-5N operations in the combat theater, three steps were taken: deicer boots for the wings and empennage; deicing systems for the propeller and windscreen. Additionally, the -5NL had

an independent G-suit system, electrically operated.

The deicer boots on the leading edge of wings, horizontal and vertical stabilizers were a simple yet effective means of limiting or even preventing accumulation of ice, which not only added weight but spoiled aerodynamic effectiveness. Power for the pneumatically-operated rubber boots was provided by an engine-driven air pump operated by a cockpit switch. Alternating inflation and deflation of parallel tubes within the boots produced a rippling motion intended to shake off accumulating ice or broke off

*F4U-5NL BuNo 124672 was accepted by the Navy on 19 March 1951 and assigned to VC-4 at NAS Atlantic City, N.J., at the end of the month. From 1951 to 1954 it made at least four deployments with various VC-4 detachments, including Det 13 in Siboney (CVE-112), Det 14 in Saipan (CVL-48), Det Bravo in Essex (CV-9), and Det Nan aboard Princeton (CV-37). The U-bird was stricken from the Navy list in March 1955 with a total of 730 flight hours. (SDAM)*

much of the ice which did form or adhere.

With the deicer boots operating, flight characteristics were essentially identical to the "straight dash five" from 105 to 240 knots. When the boots were inflated to minimize accumulation of ice on the leading edges, the airplane rolled to starboard at airspeeds over 240 and to port at speeds under 105 knots. A power-on landing was not greatly effected, as the Corsair's controls remained "satisfactory" down to 80 knots. At lesser airspeeds, greater control inputs were required, and the pilot's handbook noted that "rapid and large amounts of lateral stick displacement" were necessary to keep the wings level. Pilots were further warned to avoid landings and dives with the deicer boots operating.

Ice on a propeller was of equal concern, as the prop blades also were airfoils subject to the denigrating effects of ice. A system of deicer "shoes" on each blade and a fluid pump drew anti-icing fluid from the water injection tank and spread it onto the grooved shoes, which tended to hold the fluid so it spread outward over the surface of the blade.

A comparable arrangement was provided to prevent accumulation of windscreen ice, which could reduce or destroy forward vision from the cockpit. Three atomizer tubes installed on the windscreen drew the same deicing fluid from the water injection tank as the propeller deicing system. The pilot depressed a switch which continued pumping the fluid onto the windscreen, much the same method as windshield cleaners in modern automobiles.

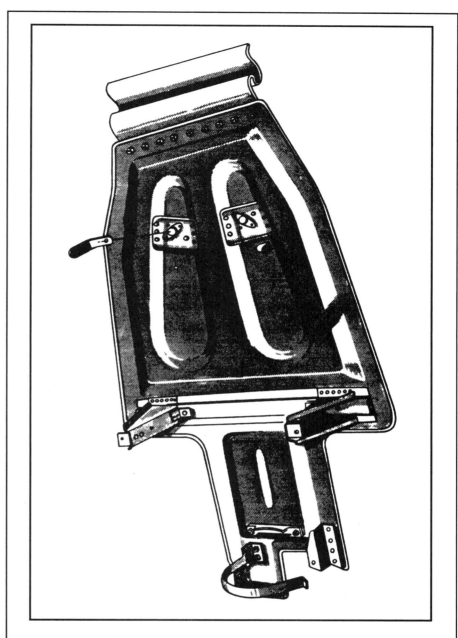

**Figure 101— Dive-brake Fairing**

*F4U main landing gear doors attach to the front of the struts and serve as dive brake fairings. According to the handbook, "A selector handle in the cockpit within reach of the pilot's left hand is both landing gear actuator and dive brake operator. Seated at the bottom of a square U-shaped channel, the handle can be pushed to the left and up to lower the gear, or to the right and up to actuate the main gear dive brakes. The brakes allow a steep dive angle without excessive speed build up, useful in bombing. When the dive brake option is selected, the tailwheel remains retracted. If actuated at high speeds, the landing gear dive brakes may hang in the slipstream, not locking until the speed diminishes sufficiently to allow the hydraulic system to force the main gear down and locked, typically at or below 225 knots." (Compton/Keller collections)*

### THE PHOTO BIRDS

The Corsair's versatility was enhanced with addition of the photographic reconnaissance mission. Though a few F4U-4Ps were produced, the Vought's primary "recce" version was the -5P, of which 30 were built. The "five Peter" was capable of carrying three types of cameras: the 12- or 24-inch focal length K-17; the 24-inch K-18; and the S-7S continuous-strip camera most useful in mapping.

The most pronounced modification to the "dash five" Corsair was installation of the camera mount behind the pilot's seat. The -5Ps were delivered with one vertical and two oblique sliding camera doors, a deflector for each door (to prevent engine oil from obscuring the image), a camera door actuating system, and a master camera switch. Installation of the camera forced the factory to relocate the remote indicating compass transmitter to the vertical stabilizer.

Depending upon the tactical requirements, a photo mission was flown with the camera either in the vertical or oblique position. Obviously, the higher the Corsair flew, the more coverage was possible on the ground. Typically, the vertically-oriented 12-inch K-17 from 15,000 feet above the ground provided half the scale of the same camera flown at 30,000 feet.

Film capacity varied greatly with the different types of cameras: from a minimum 90 exposures on a 75-foot strip in the 12-inch K-17 to 485 exposures in the same camera's 390-foot film in the 24-inch focal length model.

Recce pilots reported no significant differences in handling or performance over the standard F4U-5. Mounted near the aircraft's center of gravity, the 54.5-pound K-17 12-inch camera and the 72-pound 24-inch versions (both K-17 and K-18) were well positioned to retain the Corsair's original characteristics.

Vertical ("overhead") photo missions were usually flown at altitudes above 5,000 feet AGL at

*One of 30 F4U-5Ps, this photo-reconnaissance Corsair is discernable by the teardrop fairing on the vertical stabilizer—a change required when cameras displaced the remote inductor compass from its usual location in the fuselage. This -5P is armed with four 20 millimeters, and the few such models assigned to combat squadrons made use of cannon as well as cameras to complete their missions. The type was typically assigned to the headquarters squadron of a Marine Air Group rather than to dedicated "recce" outfits. (Peter M. Bowers)*

*Demonstrating its peculiar landing gear retraction, an F4U-5N tucks wheels in the well immediately after lifting off the runway. The port main mount already has retracted while the starboard gear has not quite rotated flush with the undersurface of the wing. The tailwheel retracted last. (SDAM)*

*BuNo 129380 parked on the ramp at MCAS Brown Field, Quantico, Virginia. Interesting to note are the four 20MM cannon and ten underwing hard points, emphasizing the "attack" in the AU-1's designation, and the small, hard rubber tailwheel intended for carrier operations. (SDAM)*

*If old soldiers never die, then old Corsairs never retire—until they have to. These Goodyear aircraft, redesignated NFG-1Ds in deference to their training status, test their engines and hydraulics at NAS Sand Point, Washington, during a Naval Air Reserve exercize in 1957.*

*Early production F4U-4 with eight HVARs. Some 2,350 dash fours were produced from early 1944 into 1946, some of which flew both in WW II and the Korean War. Though aerial combat opportunities were rare in Korea, shore- and carrier-based F4U-4s more than earned their keep in thousands of close air support and interdiction sorties against North Korean and Chinese Communist forces. (SDAM)*

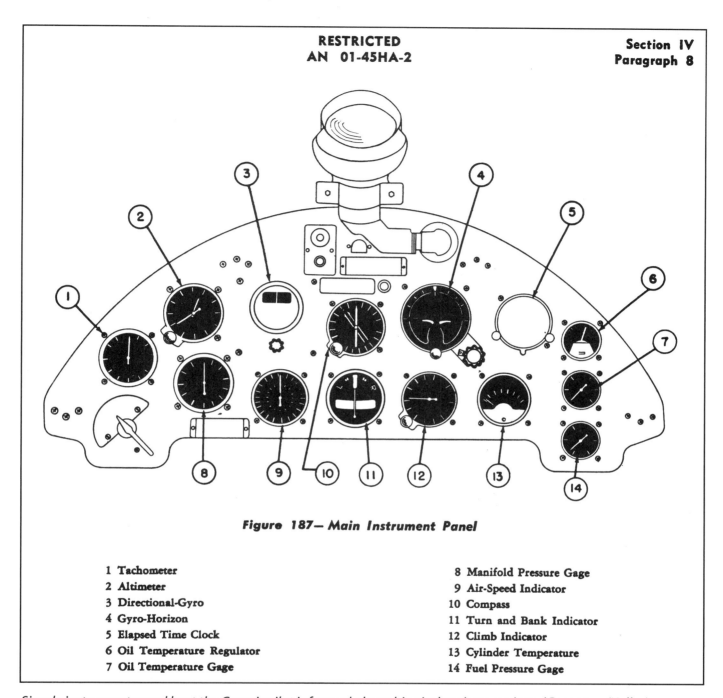

**Figure 187— Main Instrument Panel**

1 Tachometer
2 Altimeter
3 Directional-Gyro
4 Gyro-Horizon
5 Elapsed Time Clock
6 Oil Temperature Regulator
7 Oil Temperature Gage

8 Manifold Pressure Gage
9 Air-Speed Indicator
10 Compass
11 Turn and Bank Indicator
12 Climb Indicator
13 Cylinder Temperature
14 Fuel Pressure Gage

*Simple instrument panel kept the Corsair pilot informed about his airplane's operations.* (Compton/Keller)

groundspeeds of more than 220 knots. Otherwise, the shutter intervalometer settings (no faster than three seconds between shots) would not permit the desired 60% overlap considered necessary to gain full coverage. Photo missions called for extremely fine airmanship—constant speed, heading, and altitude. Ask any private pilot

how easy it is to fly "just straight and level."

Low-level photo missions were the province of oblique cameras, which permitted slanting photography either with or without a 60% overlap. For instance, a three-degree oblique angle on the 24-inch K-17 camera permitted a 280-

knot groundspeed at 400 feet while still retaining the desired overlap. Assuming that mission planners could dispense with the standard overlap, pilots could fly as low as 300 feet and 260 to 340 knots groundspeed, and could still stop motion at the maximum shutter setting.

*Enough to make a grown aviator cry. No fewer than 58 Corsairs, mostly FG-1Ds, in parade formation at Marine Corps Air Station Cherry Point, North Carolina, in September 1948. AF, CF, FF, and HF tail codes indicate the Reserve units from NRAB Anacostia; Columbus, Ohio; Jacksonville, Florida; and Miami, Florida. (Peter M. Bowers)*

*An NRAB Oakland Reserve F4U-4, BuNo 81667, with its newly-applied white N prefix and orange fuselage band. The Corsair was photographed near Benecia, California, in July 1949. (Peter M. Bowers)*

*The second production F4U-5, BuNo 121794, undergoing flight test at NAS Patuxent River, Maryland. The dash five model was tested with two converted dash fours, first flown in April 1946. Changes in the XF4U-5s were standardized in the production aircraft, built around Pratt & Whitney's R-2800-32W engine. The 223 production models began delivery in November 1947, after which Vought moved from Stratford to Dallas, Texas. Dash five production was completed there with 240 -5N night fighters between 1949 and 1951. (Peter M. Bowers)*

*Bearing a "doomsday loadout" of 984 rounds of 20MM plus eight HVARs and two huge 11.75-inch Tiny Tim rockets, this F4U-5 belongs to the commanding officer of VMA-224, circa 1950. This type of photo, so beloved of Cold War public affairs officers, actually demonstrates a configuration that was seldom carried on any occasion, and almost never in combat. (Peter M. Bowers)*

*BuNo 80760, the second "production" (i.e., unmodified) XF4U-4, with fuel tank and 500-pound bomb on the hardpoints in January 1945. Especially notable is the unusual checkerboard cowling highlighted by a yellow streamlined pattern.*

*Among the more obscure designations in the Corsair's history was the pre-production F4U-4X. Two F4U-1s were modified to "dash four" configuration, designated F4U-4XA and -XB, primarily to test installation of the C-series R-2800 engine. They were tested between April and July 1944. Three more dash one airframes were then modified to production status XF4U-4s, first flying in October of that year.*

# CORSAIRS VERSUS THE WORLD

## A TECHNICAL COMPARISON

A fascinating look at the F4U and contemporary Allied and Axis fighters was provided by retired Royal Navy Captain Eric M. Brown. A combat-experienced Grumman Martlet (Wildcat) pilot, Brown became one of the world's foremost test pilots, eventually entering some 487 aircraft types in his logbook.

His 1988 study, *Duels in the Sky*, drew the following comparisons between the Corsair and other contenders:

In the Atlantic arena, especially at low level, the Corsair II (F4U-1A) was nearly matched by the Messerschmitt 109G-6. Brown advocated a vertical fight for the German aircraft; to offset the Corsair's excellent roll rate. He concludes, "The Me-109G6...would find itself unable to afford tactical errors against the powerful American fighter."

Against the Focke-Wulf 190A-4, Brown was unequivocable: a matchup between a heavyweight and a lightweight fighter. "The FW-190A-4 was arguably the best piston-engine fighter of WW II. It is a clear winner in combat with the Corsair."

*Range was the major consideration of aircraft performance in the Pacific war, and this early 1944 F4U-1 displays installation of the standard drop rank. Depending upon mission requirements, early Corsairs could fly combat missions of 300 miles radius on internal fuel, which represented a significant improvement over the F4F-4 Wildcat. The centerline 178-gallon tank represented as much as three additional hours endurance at economy cruise, but standard procedure was to drop external tanks before engaging enemy aircraft.*

The first Corsair ace was 1st Lt. Kenneth A. Walsh, 26-year-old veteran aviator who flew with VMF-124, the first Corsair squadron in combat. First flying from Guadalcanal in early 1943, Walsh was credited with 20 victories in five months and received the Medal of Honor for two missions in August. He enlisted in the Marine Corps in 1933 and two years later entered flight training as a private. Flying a VMF-222 F4U-4, Walsh scored his 21st and last kill north of Okinawa on June 22, 1945. He retired as a lieutenant colonel in 1962.

In the Pacific, Brown paired Allied fighters with selected Japanese designs, including the Nakajima Type 2 army fighter, or "Tojo." In pure performance, Brown favored the Japanese entry by a narrow margin but conceded firepower and protection to the F4U. In the end, he believed that tactics would decide the matter, with the choice "resting largely with the Corsair."

There was a clearer verdict against the Kawasaki Type 61 "Tony" which possessed only two advantages: greater initial dive acceleration and a somewhat better turn radius.

Major Greg Boyington and four of his Black Sheep at VMF-214's operations hut, probably on Munda, New Georgia, in late 1943. Under Boyington's command the squadron claimed 96 shootdowns; 67 by eight aces, including himself. Largely unknown is the fact that the original 214 flew F4F-4 Wildcats under Major H.A. Ellis and then converted to Corsairs under W.H. Pace (KIA in August 1943). Led by Major S.R. Baily, the Black Sheep deployed in USS Franklin (CV-13) in February 1945 but "Big Ben" suffered severe kamikaze damage on the second day of operations.

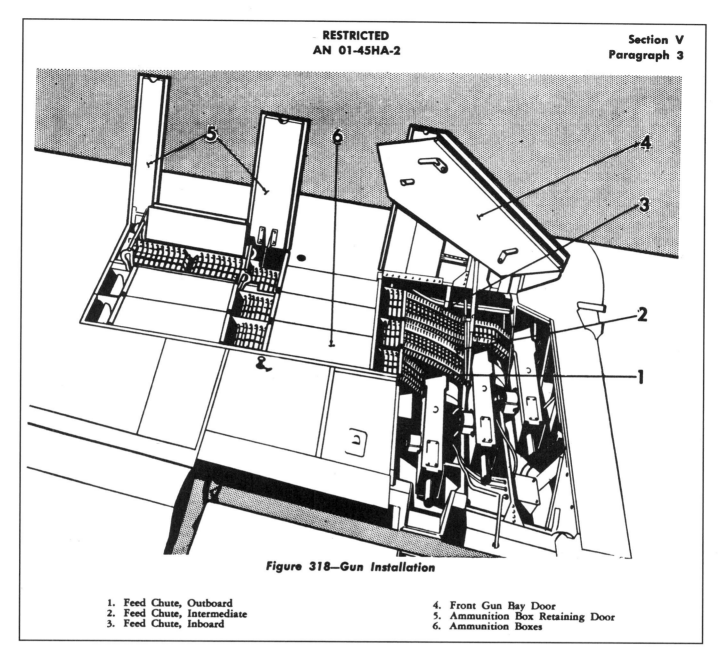

*Figure 318—Gun Installation*

1. Feed Chute, Outboard
2. Feed Chute, Intermediate
3. Feed Chute, Inboard

4. Front Gun Bay Door
5. Ammunition Box Retaining Door
6. Ammunition Boxes

*With three M-2 .50-caliber machine guns in each wing, versions of the F4U so equipped needed to stagger the gun mounts to allow access for ammunition feed to each weapon, as shown in the left wing drawing. The Corsair Erection and Maintenance manual notes: "There are six ammunition boxes, two per gun, in each outer panel, lying across the ribs outboard of the guns. Each box holds 200 rounds with the exception of the aft outboard box which, in order to fit into the wing contour, is less deep than the others and holds 175 rounds."*

By employing vertical (hit and run) tactics, the Corsair would prevail.

Japan's premier land-based naval fighter, the Kawanishi N1K2 "George," was built along Vought lines: a relatively large aircraft with a powerful engine and heavy arma-ment. In Brown's opinion, pilot skill would prove decisive: far moreso than any perceived advantages of the George.

Brown also compared the Corsair to Britain's premier naval fighter, the Supermarine Seafire Mk III. He found them evenly matched below 10,000 feet, with "only one differ-ence between these two splendid fighters," that factor being the Seafire's greater agility. However, the Corsair was more rugged, longer ranged, and far better suited to carrier operations.

*Three of VMF-215's most ambitious pilots (L-R): 1st Lt. Robert M. Hanson, Captains Harold L. Spears and Donald N. Aldrich at Bougainville in January 1944. They claimed 25, 15, and 20 planes, respectively, amounting to nearly half the squadron's total. Hanson received a Medal of Honor after his 3 February death; Spears was killed in an SBD crash at MCAS El Toro, Calif., in December 1944; and Aldrich died attempting a forced landing in an F4U-4 near Chicago in May 1947.*

*Distinctive in USS* Antietam's *(CV-36) vertical stripes, a VBF-89 Corsair taxies to its parking space at Kahului, Hawaii, circa July 1945. Air Group 89 was aboard just in time to miss the end of the war, supporting allied operations in disarming Japanese naval and land forces along the Chinese coast after the surrender in early September. (SDAM)*

In his final reckoning, "Winkle" Brown ranked the Corsair fourth among WW II naval fighters, behind the Grumman Hellcat, Mitsubishi "Zeke" and his beloved Martlet /Wildcat.

### V-J DAY AND BEYOND

When Japan capitulated on 15 August 1945, the U.S. Navy and Marine Corps had approximately 2,100 Corsairs in over 70 squadrons, including replacement training air groups ("RAGs"). Additionally, 13 Royal Navy squadrons had on strength another 255 aircraft.

The following World War Two data, including its Korean War counterpart, is based on monthly aircraft location and allowance reports, which occasionally are incomplete.

### CORSAIR SQUADRONS AUGUST 1945

Models listed in order of squadron strength

#### U.S. NAVY

VBF-1                    USS *Bennington*
28 FG-1D, F4U-1D

VBF-3                        Oceana, Va.
36 F4U-4

VBF-4                    Wildwood, N.J.
36 FG-1/1D, F4U-1/1D, F3A-1

VBF-5                Klamath Falls, Ore.
24 FG-1A, F4U-1/1C, F3A-1

VBF-6                      USS *Hancock*
36 F4U-4

VF-10                       USS *Intrepid*
33 F4U-4

*(text continued on page 69)*

# CORSAIRS IN COLOR

## CAMOUFLAGE AND MARKINGS FROM AROUND THE WORLD

The Corsair's production run spanned the early period of color photography, roughly 1940 through 1953. Because of the relative scarcity of Kodachrome film in the early 1940s, few prewar color F4U photos were taken, and not a great many more survive from the 1942-1945 era. Photographers still covet Kodachrome, which lasts almost indefinitely if protected from light. However, climate control is essential to preservation of other World War Two color film such as Ectachrome, and far too many surviving images have "faded to red" over five decades.

*Beautifully restored F4U-1D BuNo 92468 flown by former Vought executive Paul Thayer, a World War Two Navy fighter pilot. Ling Temco Vought helped fund restoration of the Corsair for the "Confederate Air Force," and added test pilot John Konrad's name to the crew list ahead of the cockpit. Unfortunately, the paint shop applied the Korean War "Navy" logo to the fuselage and VMF-312's checkerboard to the cowling—an outrageous contradiction to markings buffs.*

*Bearing transition markings from the "blue Navy to the gray Navy," this dash four has elements of both worlds: gray over white fuselage with Reserve orange stripe and blue wings with previous K designator for NRAB Olathe. (B.R. Baker via Dave Menard)*

Throughout the 1950s color photography grew in popularity, and the distinctive markings of the postwar era were captured with increasing frequency. The images presented here are typical in that respect, mainly depicting the Korean War period as well as the Naval Air Reserve's transitional markings from the "blue Navy" of the 1950s to the "gray Navy" of the early 1960s.

Most of the photos come from the files of David Menard, a staffer at the Air Force Museum in Dayton, Ohio. Dave's generosity in sharing part of his personal collection with like-minded enthusiasts is deeply appreciated.

*The French Navy's Flotille 17.F flew Corsairs from Oran, Telergma, and Bizerte during the Algerian campaign and from the British-built light carrier Arromanches in 1955-56. F4U-7s as well as transferred AU-1s saw combat under the French tricolor in Indochina and during Middle East crises of the 1950s. (Dave Menard)*

*A VF-44 Corsair raises its tail during deck-run launch from USS Boxer (CV-21) in June 1953. Fighting 44 was assigned to Air Task Group One, an air group composed of "leftover" squadrons when the standard five-squadron organization proved too large for Korean combat. (D.T. Ferrell via Tailhook)*

*Restored in French naval markings, including yellow bands used during the Suez crisis in 1956, this F4U-7 was exhibited at the Abbottsford International Air Show in British Colombia in August 1977. F4U-7s were all built after World War Two; first flight of this model was in 1952. (Frederick A. Johnsen)*

*VMF-323 F4U-4 prepares to launch from USS Sicily (CVE-118) with Lieutenant Bud Yount at the controls. Major Charlie Kunz's Corsairs worked for Sicily's skipper, Captain Jimmy Thach, from May to October 1951, providing close air support for Marines and other allied forces. (Maj. Bud Yount, USMC, via Tailhook)*

*Naval Reserve NF4U-4 of NRAB Oakland photographed over the Sacramento River by William T. Larkins in July 1949. The orange fuselage band was emblematic of the Naval Air Reserve well into the 1960s. (Dave Menard)*

*F4U-5N BuNo 124443 in South Korea, circa 1952. Assigned to VMF(N)-513, this nocturnal Corsair belonged to the Marines' most successful night fighter squadron. (Dave Menard)*

*Looking factory new, an F4U-4 on the transit line of Coriapolis Army Air Field, Pennsylvania, in 1945. Visible markings do not permit identification of the unit, though several Navy air groups were on the East Coast at war's end, preparing for the expected invasion of Japan. (William J. Balogh, Sr., via Dave Menard)*

*The Canadian Warplane Heritage's Goodyear-built FG-1D was painted in New Zealand markings when photographed at Oshkosh in 1978. Yellow patches over gun muzzles keep air from ramming into wing cavities, and may have added efficiency; firing the guns would break the seal, when such patches were used on operational air craft. (Frederick A. Johnsen)*

*Little known even among American warbird enthusiasts is this F4U-4 displayed at Seoul, Republic of Korea. Restored in VMA-312 markings, the checkerboard Corsair is periodically rolled out for military demonstrations as a tribute to Marine Corps aviators who defended the ROK from northern aggression. (Dave Menard)*

(text continued from page 64)

VBF-10 USS                  *Intrepid*
36 F4U-4

VBF-14              Kahului, Hawaii
38 F4U-4, F4U-1D, FG-1D

VBF-15              Los Alamitos, Cal.
18 F4U-1/1D, FG-1, F3A-1

VBF-19               Alameda, Cal.
47 F4U-4, F4U-1/1D, F3A-1, FG-1A

VBF-20              Edenton, N.C.
38 F4U-4

VF-74A               Otis Field
23 F4U-4, F4U-1

VF-74B               Otis Field
24 F4U-4, F4U-1/1D, FG-1D

VBF-74A             Otis Field
15 F4U-4, F4U-1D

VBF-74B             Otis Field
24 F4U-4, F4U-1D, FG-1D

VF-75A              Chincoteague, Va.
20 F4U-4

VF-75B              Chincoteague, Va.
24 F4U-4

VBF-75A            Wildwood, N.J.
22 F4U-1/1D, FG-1/1D

VBF-75B            Wildwood, N.J.
24 F4U-1/1D, FG-1/1D, F3A-1

VBF-80             Holtville, Cal.
36 FG-1D, F4U-1/1D, F4U-4

VBF-81              Pasco, WA
34 F4U-1/1D, FG-1/1A, F3A-1

VBF-83              USS *Essex*
35 FG-1D, F4U-1D

Two F4U-4s of VBF-6 from USS Hancock (CV-19) in the Western Pacific in the summer of 1945. The fighter-bomber designation originated in January that year, mainly as a means of easing administrative workload for enlarged carrier squadrons of 110 pilots and 73 aircraft. The U tail code replaced "Hanna's" previous horse shoe air group "G" symbol in June, when VBF-6 traded in its FG-1Ds for dash fours.

Widely considered "Mister Corsair" in the U.S. Navy was Commander Tom Blackburn, skipper of VF-17 in 1943-44 and later Commander Air Group 75 aboard USS Midway (CVB-41) in 1945-46. Here, aloft in his CAG bird, Blackburn supervises a "group grope" with some of the 90 Corsairs of VF-75A and B, and VBF-75A and B. Additionally, Midway was to have embarked 48 SBF-4 or SBW-4 Helldivers of Bombing 75 and Torpedo 75. In the end, however, the huge air group proved unmanageable, and a more streamlined table of organization was established. (SDAM)

| VBF-84 | Los Alamitos, Cal. | VBF-88 | USS *Yorktown* | VBF-94 | USS *Lexington* |
|---|---|---|---|---|---|
| 33 F4U-4, F4U-1/1D, F3A-1, FG-1D | | 37 FG-1D | | 32 F4U-4 | |

| VBF-85 | USS *Shangri La* | VBF-89 | USS *Antietam* | VBF-95 | Hilo, Hawaii |
|---|---|---|---|---|---|
| 34 FG-1D, F4U-1D | | 37 F4U-4 | | 39 F4U-4, F4U-1/1D, FG-1D | |

| VBF-86 | USS *Wasp* | VBF-93 | USS *Boxer* | VBF-97 | Grosse Ile, Mich. |
|---|---|---|---|---|---|
| 36 F4U-4 | | | 37 F4U-4 | 16 F4U-1/1D, FG-1, F3A-1 | |

VBF-98       San Diego & Thermal
58 F4U-1/1D, FG-1/1A

VBF-99       Saipan
38 F4U-1/1D, F4U-4, FG-1D

VBF-100       Barbers Pt., Hawaii
40 F4U-1/1D, FG-1D, F4U-4

VBF-150       USS *Lake Champlain*
35 F4U-4

VBF-151 Corvallis, Ore.       1 FG-1A

VBF-152       Groton & Manteo
37 F4U-4

VBF-153       Manteo & Oceana
36 F4U-4

38 USN squadrons; 1,236 Corsairs

*Flying a stepped-down formation on their division leader, three F4U-1Ds of VMF-323 return to Kadena Airfield after a close air support mission on Okinawa in 1945. The Death Rattlers emerged as the champion killers of the Tactical Air Force, with 124.5 confirmed victories over Japanese aircraft, including six by the CO, Major George C. Axtell who formed and led the squadron for nearly two years. Eleven other Rattlers also became aces during the campaign.* (Peter M. Bowers)

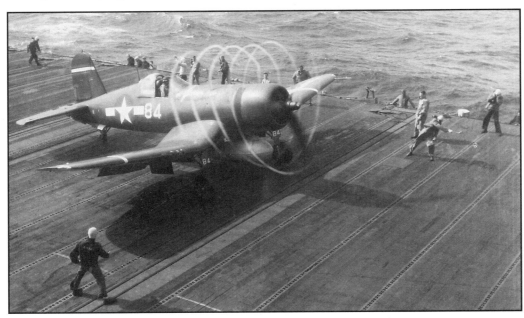

*Weaving a spiral halo, a Marine aviator receives the go signal from USS Essex's (CV-9) flight deck officer. Marine Corsairs began routine carrier operations in late December 1944 as VMF-124 and -213 joined the Navy's Air Group Four in the Western Pacific. Called to fleet service in response to the worsening kamikaze crisis, Lieutenant Colonel William Millington's two squadrons incurred heavy losses to overcome the hazards of carrier flying and adverse weather. They paved the way for eight more Leatherneck F4U squadrons operating with the Fast Carrier Task Force before the war's end.* (Peter M. Bowers)

VMF-111                                    Engebi
24 F4U-1/1D

VMF-113                                    Ie Shima
36 F4U-1D, FG-1D

VMF-115                              Zamboanga, PI
23 FG-1/1D, F4U-1D

VMF-121                             Peleliu & Ulithi
30 FG-1/1D, F4U-1D

VMF-122                                    Peleliu
24 F4U-1D, FG-1D

VMF-155                         Roi, Majuro & Kwaj.
20 F4U-1D

VMF-211                              Zamboanga, PI
24 F4U-1D, FG-1D

VMF-212                             Awase, Okinawa
36 F4U-4

VMF-215                               Ewa, Hawaii
25 FG-1/1D, F4U-1D, F4U-4

VMF-218                              Zamboanga, PI
22 FG-1/1D, F4U-1D

VMF-222                             Anase, Okinawa
32 F4U-4

VMF-223                             Awase, Okinawa
31 F4U-4

VMF-224                             Chimu, Okinawa
31 F4U-1D, FG-1D

VMF-311                             Chimu, Okinawa
32 F4U-1C

VMF-312                             Awase, Okinawa
31 FG-1D, F4U-1D

VMF-314                                   Ie Shima
32 F4U-1C

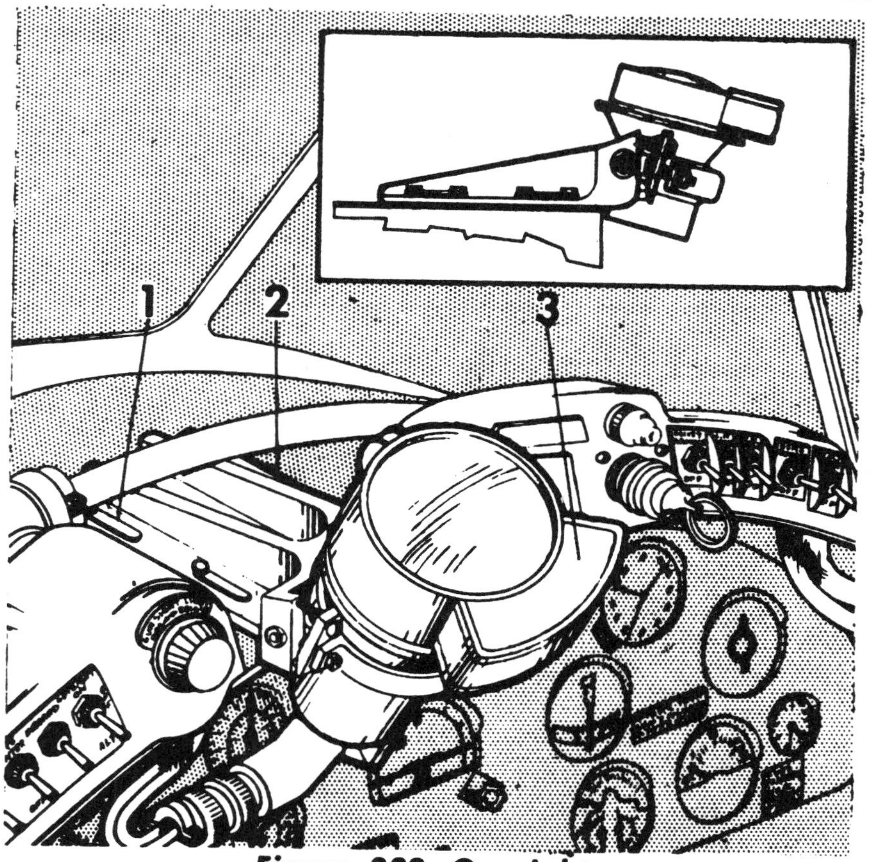

**Figure 323—Gunsight**

1.  Slots
2.  Mounting Bracket
3.  Crash Pad

*Centrally mounted Mark 8 gunsight had a rubber crash pad to protect the pilot.* (Compton/Keller)

VMF-322           Kadena, Okinawa
33 FG-1D, F4U-1D

VMF-323           Kadena, Okinawa
32 FG-1D, F4U-1D

VMF-324                     Midway
27 FG-1

VMF-351     USS *Cape Gloucester* 18
FG-1D (+2 F6F-5P)

VMF-422                    Ie Shima
32 F4U-1D, FG-1D

VMF-441            Chimu, Okinawa
32 F4U-1C/1D, FG-1D

VMF-461                   El Toro, Cal.
18 FG-1A

VMF-462                   El Toro, Cal.
34 FG-1, F4U-1, F3A-1

VMF-471                   El Toro, Cal.
35 FG-1, F3A-1

VMF-481             Santa Barbara, Cal.
#s Unknown

VMF-511             USS *Block Island*
10 FG-1D, F4U-1D (+ 10 F6F-5N/P)

VMF-512            USS *Gilbert Islands*
18 FG-1D, F4U-1D (+ 1 F6F-5P)

Another first production block airplane, BuNo 02288 served with VMF-214 in the Solomon Islands during June 1943. This photo was taken at Guadalcanal during the squadron's first combat tour, prior to its incarnation as Major Greg Boyington's famous Black Sheep. Under Captain G.F. Britt and Major H.A. Ellis, the squadron claimed 30 victories in Wildcats and Corsairs between March and September 1943. The first VMF-214 produced two aces: Lieutenants Alvin Jensen (6) and Hartwell Scarborough (5). (Peter M. Bowers)

The Hell's Angels emblem of VMF-321 undoubtedly owed its inspiration to the famous 3rd Squadron of the American Volunteer Group in China and Burma during 1941-42. Arriving at Bougainville on Christmas Eve 1943, Major J.M. Miller's angels were credited with 39.66 aerial victories while producing one ace, Lieutenant R.B. See with five. The squadron later flew from Green Island and Guam before returning to the U.S. in late 1944. At war's end VMF-321 was aboard USS Puget Sound (CVE-113), possibly the ship where this Corsair is chocked and tied down. The Hell's Angels still exist as a Marine Reserve F/A-18 squadron. (Peter M. Bowers)

| VMF-513 | USS *Vella Gulf* |
|---|---|
| 16 F4U-1D (+ 2 F6F-5P) | |

| VMF-521 | Congaree, S.C. |
|---|---|
| c. 18 FG-1A, F3A-1 | |

| VMF-522 | Congaree, S.C. |
|---|---|
| c. 23 FG-1A, F3A-1 | |

| VMF-523 | Congaree, S.C. |
|---|---|
| c. 22 FG-1A, F3A-1 | |

| VMF-524 | Parris I., S.C. |
|---|---|
| c. 24 FG-1A, F3A-1 | |

| VMF-911 | Cherry Pt., S.C. |
|---|---|
| #s Unknown | |

| VMF-913 | Cherry Pt., S.C. |
|---|---|
| c. 24 FG-1A, F3A-1 | |

| VMF-914 | Greenville, S.C. |
|---|---|
| c. 23 FG-1A, F3A-1 | |

34-36 squadrons; c. 874 Corsairs

In August 1945, many Marine fighting squadrons were equipped with F6F Hellcats or were reforming with temporarily-assigned SBN/SBW Helldivers. Therefore, some prominent squadrons (i.e., VMF-124, 213, and 214) are not represented in this accounting.

### Royal Navy

| No. 1831 Sqn. | HMS *Glory* |
|---|---|
| 21 Corsair IV (FG-1A/1D) | |

| No. 1834 Sqn. | HMS *Victorious* |
|---|---|
| 18 Corsair II (F4U-1A) & IV | |

| No. 1835 Sqn. | Belfast |
|---|---|
| 21 Corsair IV | |

| No. 1836 Sqn. | HMS *Victorious* |
|---|---|
| 18 Corsair II & IV | |

| No. 1837 Sqn. | Nutts Corner |
|---|---|
| 21 Corsair III (F3A-1A) | |

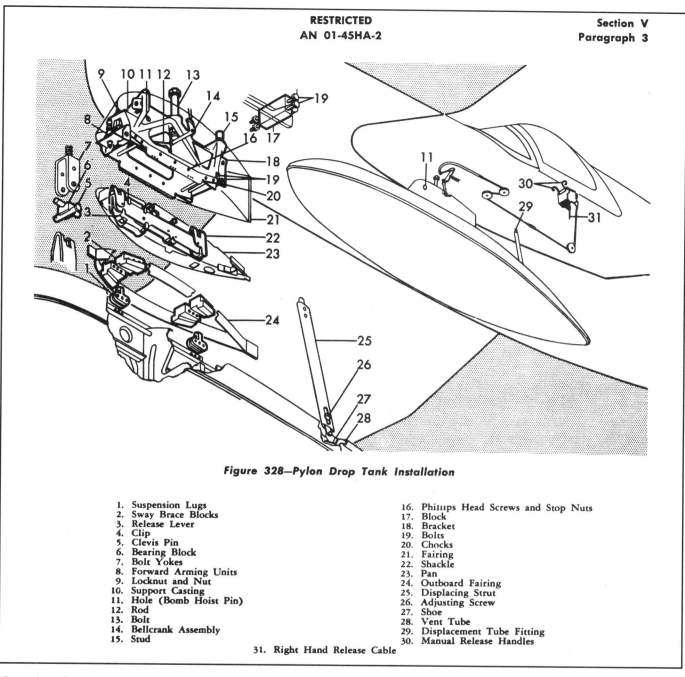

**Figure 328—Pylon Drop Tank Installation**

1. Suspension Lugs
2. Sway Brace Blocks
3. Release Lever
4. Clip
5. Clevis Pin
6. Bearing Block
7. Bolt Yokes
8. Forward Arming Units
9. Locknut and Nut
10. Support Casting
11. Hole (Bomb Hoist Pin)
12. Rod
13. Bolt
14. Bellcrank Assembly
15. Stud
16. Phillips Head Screws and Stop Nuts
17. Block
18. Bracket
19. Bolts
20. Chocks
21. Fairing
22. Shackle
23. Pan
24. Outboard Fairing
25. Displacing Strut
26. Adjusting Screw
27. Shoe
28. Vent Tube
29. Displacement Tube Fitting
30. Manual Release Handles
31. Right Hand Release Cable

*Corsair pylon installation for drop tanks included a displacing strut (part 25) to ensure drop tank cleared the aircraft's structure without striking it when released. Manual release cables culminated in two release handles (part 30) in cockpit.*

| No. 1841 Sqn. 18 Corsair IV | HMS *Formidable* | No. 1846 Sqn. 21 Corsair IV | HMS *Colossus* | No. 1852 Sqn. 21 Corsair IV | Belfast |
| No. 1842 Sqn. 18 Corsair IV | HMS *Formidable* | No. 1850 Sqn. 21 Corsair IV | HMS *Vengeance* | No. 1853 Sqn. 18 Corsair IV | Machrihanish |
| No. 1845 Sqn. 18 Corsair IV | Nowra | No. 1851 Sqn. 21 Corsair IV | HMS *Venerable* | 13 RN squadrons, 255 Corsairs | |

# KOREAN AND OTHER WARS

## LATE F4U AND AU-1 USE

The Corsair was indispensable to naval aviation's three-year effort in Korea. Every carrier which deployed to Task Force 77 between June 1950 and July 1953 had at least a detachment of night fighters or photo-recce U-birds, but more often Corsairs were represented in squadron strength.

One big-deck air group was entirely "jet free" during Korean War combat deployments, reflecting the importance of strike and interdiction in that "conflict." With limited strike potential, F9F Panthers flew more sorties than any other carrier aircraft during the war (primarily CAPs) but carried less ordnance. Consequently, during *Boxer's* (CV-21) 1950 cruise, lasting from late August to mid-November, Air Group Two embarked its own VF-23 and 24 plus VF-63 and 64 "on loan" from CAG-6. Additionally, VA-65's AD-2 Skyraiders rounded out the all-propeller air group, with Corsair photo birds and night fighters plus Skyraider night heckler and elec-

tronic warfare detachments.

Owing to the press of events on the Korean peninsula, Air Group Two conducted a head-spinning three-week turnaround before the end of 1950. Leaving *Boxer* on 11 November, CAG D.M. White turned over to Commander R.W. Rynd who took the group aboard *Valley Forge* (CV-45) on 6 December. The same four Corsair squadrons remained in the lineup when "Happy Valley" returned to the West Coast on 7 April 1951.

*A VF-791 F4U-4 weaves a vapor trail in humid air aboard USS* Boxer *(CV-21) prior to launch in July 1951. "Dot" is armed with 100-pound antipersonnel bombs on the outer racks, plus fuel and/or napalm tanks under the wing stubs. Lieutenant Commander J.B. Kisner's Reserve squadron flew with Air Group 101 from March to October that year. (SDAM)*

Scores of Corsairs—mostly FG-1s—awaiting disposition at Litchfield, Arizona, circa 1955. Discernable markings indicate that nearly all came from Naval Air Reserve units from as far away as New York State. Most of these aircraft were eventually scrapped, but some reached private hands and a few again flew as military aircraft in Latin American air forces. (SDAM)

A VF-53 F4U-4 during a deck-run takeoff from USS Essex (CV-9) on 3 March 1952. Contrast this lighter ordnance load with those of land-based Marine Corsairs: even with catapult assistance, there was seldom enough wind over the deck to launch F4Us with comparable loadouts to their land-based partners. (SDAM)

*The Black Sheeps' second war was fought off Korea as VMF-214 flew from USS Sicily (CVE-118). This F4U-4B is readied for a predawn launch with four 20MM cannon, eight high-velocity aerial rockets, and a 500-pound general purpose bomb. From July 1950 to February 1951 the Black Sheep had four commanding officers, including Lieutenant Colonel W.E. Lischeid who was killed in action in September. (Peter M. Bowers)*

*A VF-74 F4U-4 about to "trap" aboard USS Bon Homme Richard (CVA-31) in October 1952. This was midway through Air Group Seven's Korean War deployment which lasted from May of that year until early January 1953. Commander C.D. Fonvielle's Corsairs, though designated fighters, served wholly as attack aircraft while the F9F-2s of VF-71 and 72 provided combat air patrol. (Peter M. Bowers)*

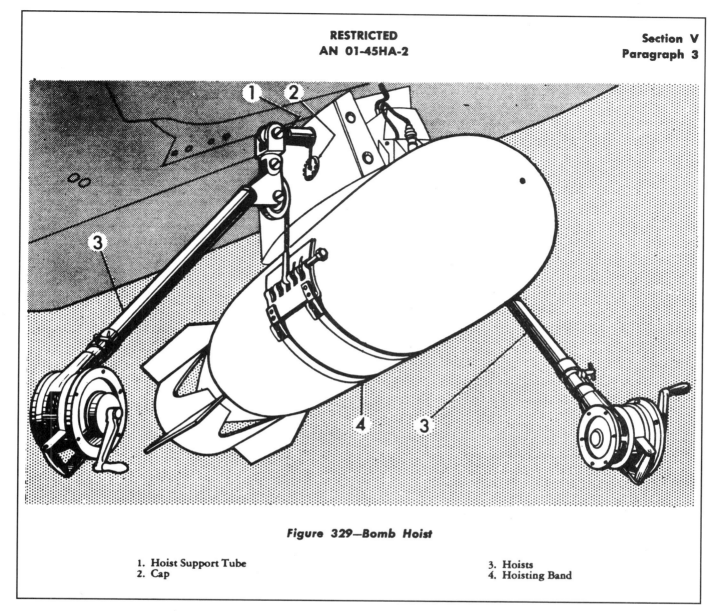

**Figure 329—Bomb Hoist**

1. Hoist Support Tube
2. Cap
3. Hoists
4. Hoisting Band

*Hand-cranked bomb hoists were available to raise ordnance up to the Corsair's mounting shackles.*
(Compton/Keller)

However, CAG-2 remained on the job, switching to *Philippine Sea* (CV-47) in March and remaining until June 1951. Though still optimized for close air support and interdiction, the organization was reduced from four fighter outfits to three: retaining VF-24 while VF-63 and 64 returned again. As before, combined with VA-65's AD-2 Skyraiders, plus the special-mission F4Us and ADs, there were no jets aboard "Phil Sea" during that midwar cruise.

Marine Corps F4U-4 and -4Bs also flew from carriers during the war, providing badly-needed close air support to leatherneck riflemen. A dozen CVE/CVL deployments included five Marine Corsair squadrons from 1950 to 1953, most notably VMF/VMA-312 with six cruises aboard *Bataan* (CVL-29), *Bairoko* (CVE-115), *Badoeng Strait* (CVE-116), and *Sicily* (CVE-118) between 1951 and 1953.

VMF-212 operated from *Bataan*, *Badoeng Strait*, and *Rendova* (CVE-114) during 1950-1952.

The Death Rattlers of VMF-323 alternated shore and sea duty, flying from *Sicily* and *Badoeng Strait* during 1950 and 1951.

Finally, VMF-214 logged a seven-month tour in Captain Jimmy Thach's *Sicily* from July 1950 to February 1951, and VMA-332 flew from

*Point Cruz* (CVE-119) from April 1953 to well beyond the armistice in July.

At the end of hostilities in July 1953, the only Marine Corsair squadron designated a fighter unit was VMFN-114, which flew -5Ns at Cherry Point. By then, the Douglas F3D Skyknight had taken over the night fighter role, and the remaining Leatherneck Corsair units were designated VMA, or attack squadrons.

## CORSAIR SQUADRONS JULY 1950

### U.S. NAVY

| Squadron | Base | Aircraft |
|---|---|---|
| VC-3 | Mofett Field, Cal. | 12 F4U-5N |
| VC-4 | Atlantic City, N.J. | 58 F4U-5N (incl. deployed) |
| VC-61 | Miramar, Cal. | 4 F4U-4P |
| VC-62 | Atlantic City, N.J. | 6 F4U-5P |
| VF-13 | Jacksonville, Fla. | 19 F4U-5 |
| VF-14 | Jacksonville, Fla. | 19 F4U-5 |
| VF-22 | Oceana, Va. | 18 F4U-4 |
| VF-23 | Oceana, Va. | 20 F4U-4 |
| VF-24 | Oceana, Va. | 18 F4U-4 |
| VF-32 | USS *Leyte* | 15 F4U-4 |
| VF-33 | USS *Leyte* | 15 F4U-4 |
| VF-53 | USS *Valley Forge* | 12 F4U-4/4B |
| VF-54 | USS *Valley Forge* | 11 F4U-4/-4B |
| VF-63 | Oceana, Va. | 15 F4U-4 |
| VF-64 | Oceana, Va. | 20 F4U-4 |

*"Whiskey Sugar Seven" was an F4U-4B of VMFA-323, ready for a mission in South Korea circa 1952. Heavy ordnance appears to be 500-pound bombs on both pylons with four 250s beneath the wings, indicating a strike mission rather than support of ground troops. The "Death Rattlers" had been the top-scoring squadron of the Okinawa-based Tactical Air Force in 1945, and in Korea rotated between shore and sea duty, flying from two escort carriers. (SDAM)*

*BuNo 97341 was Whiskey Uncle One belonging to the skipper of VMF-235 when the F4U-4s arrived in Hawaii aboard the USS Cape Esperance (CVE-88) in March, 1952. A total of 44 Corsairs were unloaded at Pearl Harbor and then flew to Kaneohe, the nearby Marine air station reactivated for service during the Korean War. This view gives an excellent perspective on how the Corsair's 41-foot wingspan was reduced to some 17 feet to fit in the narrow confines of an aircraft carrier elevator.*

*The last of seven Korean War carrier deployments by Marine F4U squadrons was VMA-332 aboard USS Point Cruz (CVE-119) beginning in April, 1953. Though hostilities ceased in late July, the colorful Polka Dots remained on station until mid-December with their F4U-4Bs. This was also the final carrier cruise for any Marine Corsair squadron, and among the last deployments for Leatherneck propeller aircraft. Marine AD Skyraider squadrons embarked in three carriers from 1954 to 1956, after which an era passed in naval aviation.*

Vought factory photo of a French Navy F4U-7, the potent fighter bomber built solely for the Aeronavale. Derived from the AU-1, with four 20mm cannon and ten underwing hard points for ordnance, the dash seven was the ultimate expression of the Corsair line. French aviators flew their F4Us in combat both in Algeria and during the Suez crisis of 1956 before accepting the next generation fighter in 1964: Vought's spectacular F-8E(FN) Crusader, still active in the fleet more than 30 years later.

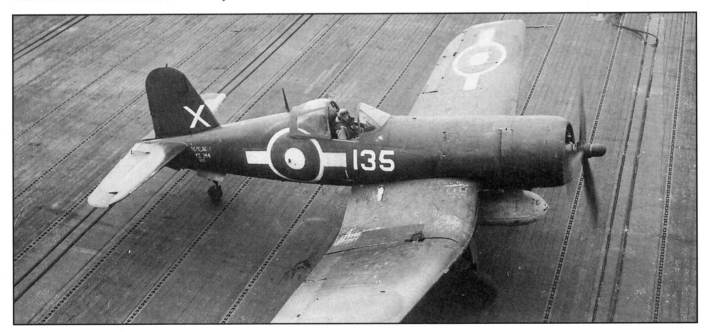

Just recovered aboard USS Shangri-La (CV-38), an HMS Formidable Corsair IV (FG-1) taxis forward over lowered barriers. The British fighter belonged to No. 1842 Squadron, one of 14 Corsair units in the Fleet Air Arm at the end of World War Two.

**WARBIRDTECH**
S E R I E S

| | | | |
|---|---|---|---|
| VF-73 | Jacksonville, Fla.<br>19 F4U-4 | VMF-214 | El Toro, Cal.<br>18 F4U-4B |
| VF-113 | San Diego, Cal.<br>21 F4U-4B | VMF-223 | Cherry Point, S.C.<br>24 F4U-4 |
| VF-114 | San Diego, Cal.<br>14 F4U-4B | VMF-225 | Cherry Point, S.C.<br>26 F4U-4 |
| VF-173 | USS *Coral Sea*<br>17 F4U-5 | VMF-311 | El Toro, Cal.<br>7 F4U-4B |
| VF-174 | USS *Coral Sea*<br>17 F4U-4/5 | VMF-312 | El Toro, Cal.<br>17 F4U-4B |

20 squadrons, 370 F4Us

VMF-323 — El Toro, Cal. 22 F4U-4B

**U.S. Marine Corps**

VMFN-114 — Cherry Point, S.C. 22 F4U-5N

| VMF-211 | Cherry Point, S.C.<br>24 F4U-4 |
|---|---|
| VMF-212 | Cherry Point, S.C.<br>37 F4U-4/5 |

VMFN-513 — El Toro, Cal. 16 F4U-5N

10 squadrons, 223 F4Us

## Corsair Squadrons July 1953

**U.S. Navy**

| VC-3 | Moffett Field, Cal.<br>31 F4U-5N/NL (incl. deployed) |
|---|---|
| VC-4 | Atlantic City, N.J.<br>26 F4U-5N/NL |
| VF-13 | USS *F.D. Roosevelt*<br>16 F4U-5 |
| VF-14 | USS F.D. *Roosevelt*<br>15 F4U-5 |
| VF-42 | Oceana, Va.<br>16 F4U-4 |
| VF-44 | USS *Boxer*<br>16 F4U-4 |
| VF-74 | Quonset Point, R.I.<br>15 F4U-4 |

Among Brewster-built aircraft was BuNo 04711, which became Corsair III JS 491, delivered to the Royal Navy circa March 1944. This F3A-1 seems to have retained its standard three-tone camouflage with British insignia applied at the factory, though the scalloped dark spot on the rudder (roughly the height of the fin flash) is nonstandard and may be fabric repair. Interesting to note is the fact that the U.S. Navy serial is retained in the usual position on the vertical fin with the RN number repeated below it. (Peter M. Bowers)

*A Vought Corsair Mark II (F4U-1D) in flight, probably on the East Coast. Royal Navy serial JT 505 explains the "505" ferry number on the cowling. The British accepted 510 Mark IIs, which first entered combat in April 1944 during strikes against the German battleship Tirpitz in Norway. (Frederick G. Freeman via Peter M. Bowers)*

| | | |
|---|---|---|
| VF-94 | USS *Philippine Sea* | |
| | 4 F4U-4 | |
| VF-104 | USS *Saipan* | |
| | 15 F4U-5 | |
| VF-152 | USS *Princeton* | |
| | 15 F4U-4 | |
| 10 squadrons, 169 F4Us | | |

**U.S. MARINE CORPS**

| | |
|---|---|
| VMFN-114 | Cherry Point, S.C. |
| | 16 F4U-5N/NL |
| VMA-312 | Miami, Fla. |
| | 15 F4U-4 |
| VMA-324 | Miami, Fla. |

| | | |
|---|---|---|
| | | 5 F4U-5 |
| VMA-324 | Pacific deployment | |
| | 23 F4U-4/4B | |
| VMA-331 | USS *Bennington* | |
| | 24 F4U-4 | |
| VMA-332 | Miami, Fla. | |
| | 1 F4U-4 | |
| VMA-333 | Miami, Fla. | |
| | 23 F4U-4 | |
| 7 squadrons, 107 F4Us | | |

**KOREAN WAR RESERVE SQUADRONS**

The following eight Naval Air Reserve squadrons flew F4U-4s during 11 Korean combat deployments, 1951-53:

| | |
|---|---|
| VF-653 | *Valley Forge*, 1951-52 |
| VF-713 | *Antietam* 1951-52 |
| VF-783 | *Bon Homme Richard*, 1951 |
| VF-791 | *Boxer*, 1951 |
| VF-821 | *Princeton*, 1951 |
| VF-871 | *Princeton*, 1951; *Essex*, 1952-3 |
| VF-874 | *Bon Homme Richard*, 1951; *Oriskany* 1952-53 (Redes. VF-124) |
| VF-884 | *Boxer*, 1951; *Kearsarge* 1952-53 (Redes. VF-144) |

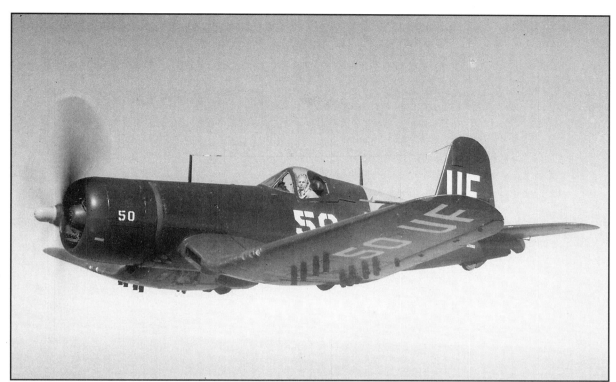

*"Uniform Foxtrot Five-Zero," a near-pristine FG-1D of St. Louis's Naval Air Reserve unit. Goodyear-built Corsairs equipped a large portion of NRAB organizations between 1945 and 1950.*

*The 40th production F4U-7, BuNo 133693, on the ramp at Dallas awaiting delivery to France. Unusual is placement of the aircraft type and serial number, immediately forward of the horizontal stabilizer instead of in the standard position below the stabilizer. (Peter M. Bowers)*

## FOREIGN SHORES

Corsairs flew in the colors of several nations allied to the United States, participating in two separate wars and assorted other international incidents. The major use, of course, occurred with the British Royal Navy and Royal New Zealand Air Force during World War Two. French naval aviation (*Aeronavale*) had its own Corsair variant, the F4U-7, which saw limited service in the Suez crisis of 1956 and during operations in Tunisia.

Latin American users included Argentina, which boasted its own carrier, plus warring enemies Honduras and El Salvador. In fact, the latter two disputed in the "Soccer War" of 1969, which proved the Corsair's last combat employment.

## BRITISH ACCENT

Lacking an indigenous single-seat carrier fighter of its own, the Royal Navy already had absorbed Grumman F4F Wildcats (originally called Martlets in RN service) as early as 1940. Large quantities of F6F Hellcats (Gannets) followed, as did 1,967 Corsairs, which were known only by their American name.

Britain's original batch of U-birds were 95 F4U-1s designated Corsair Is in 1943, with 510 Corsair IIs (F4U-1A/Ds) thereafter. They were followed by 430 Corsair IIIs (Brewster F3A-1As) and 942 Mark IVs (Goodyear FG-1A/Ds).

The first RN Corsair unit was No. 1830 Squadron, formed at NAS Quonset Point, Rhode Island, in June 1943. Eventually the Fleet Air Arm established 18 other Corsair squadrons, most of which operated from combat-deployed aircraft carriers. Corsairs remained in FAA carrier squadrons for a year after the war, finally retiring in August 1946.

Unlike the early Martlets, which were built to British specifications, the Corsairs generally retained American instruments and equipment. The exceptions were installation of British VHF radios and addition of small airscoops intended to

*Taking off from HMS* Smiter, *a Corsair launches just too late for action.* Smiter, *built in America as CVE-52, became operational in August 1945 and arrived in the East Indies before she or her aircraft could deploy for combat. Like her 37 sisters, she was returned to the U.S. in 1946 and reverted to her original merchant configuration. (Peter M. Bowers)*

A Kiwi Corsair I takes off from a Solomon Islands airfield in 1944. Some 425 U-birds were provided to the Royal New Zealand Air Force, which eventually had more than a dozen Corsair squadrons. They were employed almost exclusively in ground attack missions, supporting allied troops in the Bougainville campaign and beyond. The last RNZAF Corsairs left service in 1949. (SDAM)

A Corsair Mark IV in the Royal Navy's Fleet Air Arm Museum at Yeovilton. Markings buffs will note the nonstandard tricolor cockade on top of the folded wing, with a white middle ring more commonly found on the fuselage and undersurface rather than the red and blue variety. (Fred Johnsen)

*Glistening Corsair Mark IVs (FG-1s) at Goodyear's Akron, Ohio, factory. Contrary to some reports, the clipped wingtips were done at the plant rather than by British units after delivery, as had been the case with Corsair Is (F4U-1s). Brewster-built F3A-1s were designated Mark IIIs in the Fleet Air Arm.(SDAM)*

*Bearing British Pacific Fleet cockades—a combination of U.S. and Royal Navy emblems—this Corsair Mark II (F4U-1A/1D)from HMS Victorious taxies up the deck of USS Essex (CV-9) in early August 1945. Overall color scheme is medium gray upper surfaces and light gray under, with a cartoon character on the right side of the nose.*

prevent accumulation of carbon monoxide behind the cockpit.

The most visible change to FAA Corsairs was clipping the wingtips. Many British F4Us had eight inches cropped from each wingtip to accommodate the lower overhead on Royal Navy carriers' hangar decks, with wings folded. As designed and built, the F4U-1/1A measured 16 feet, 6 inches vertically (plus/minus a half inch) with the wings fully folded over the canopy. However, at the top of the arc while folding the wings, the Corsair required 18 feet, 3 inches, of vertical clearance. FAA pilots reported two byproducts of the modification: a somewhat higher stall speed with a crisper "payoff," and an increased roll rate owing to the 16-inch shorter wingspan.

The Royal Navy, first to use Corsairs aboard ship, also was present at the end of the war as the British Pacific Fleet launched strikes against Japan itself. Shortly before Tokyo surrendered, in August 1945, a Fleet Air Arm Corsair pilot was awarded the last Victoria Cross of World War Two. Sub-Lieutenant Robert Hampton Gray, a Canadian in HMS *Formidable's* No. 1831 Squadron, received the award posthumously for a low-level attack on a Japanese naval vessel.

At war's end the Royal Navy had 255 Corsairs in 13 squadrons. Of those, 10 whole squadrons and portions of two others flew Mark IVs. On VJ-Day eight units were embarked in six RN carriers.

Some 425 Corsair Is were allotted to the New Zealand air force, eventually serving in more than a dozen squadrons. The original Kiwi Corsair squadron in combat was No. 20 RNZAF, which began flying from Bougainville in May 1944. Their operational career almost exclusively involved land-based combat in the Solomon Islands, but included operations on Borneo as well as postwar occupation duty in Japan. The last RNZAF Corsairs were retired from service in 1949.

New Zealand Corsair squadrons in combat were Numbers 14 through 26 inclusive, supported by No. 4 Operational Training Unit and various maintenance organizations.

### FRENCH ACCENT: THE F4U-7

France's postwar modernization program included 94 F4U-7s, an outgrowth of the ground-attack AU-1 model (XF4U-6) produced wholly for the U.S. Marine Corps.

After World War Two, French naval aviation was badly in need of modern combat aircraft. The F4U-7 was the service's first new type since 1945, as previous fighters were Seafire Mk IIIs "straight from the junkyard on the basis of one for flight and two for spare," according to one senior aviator. Veteran F6F-

*Smoking tires announce an AU-1's touchdown on Patuxent River's simulated carrier deck as the Naval Air Test Center evaluates the type's carrier suitability during September 1952. The type hardly ever operated from flattops, but as a tailhook airplane, had to be certified for embarked use. (SDAM)*

5s with 2,000 flight hours at time of delivery to *Aeronavale* also left something to be desired.

Consequently, the AU-1 was upgraded with the R-2800-18W engine, and the dash sevens were delivered in two production batches: BuNos 133652-731 and 133819-832. The last ones rolled off the Dallas assembly line in December 1952.

Aside from brand-new airframes, the dash seven Corsairs arrived with a full set of spare parts, tools, and support equipment for four squadrons, two air stations, and two carriers.

Though a generation of American carrier pilots considered the F4U-7 heavy and less responsive than earlier models, their French counterparts were enthusiastic. Power folding wings and a modern, pilot-ori-ented cockpit also enhanced the new U-bird's reputation in French service.

Combat operations were relatively limited, but were far flung. In 1954, Flotille 14.F moved from the air station at Karouba, Tunisia, to support the French Army at Dien Bien Phu, French Indochina. No carrier was then available, so squadron personnel were airlifted by French airliners and American C-124s to Tourane (later Danang). The F4U-7s were left at Karouba, requiring resupply of American AU-1s from Marine Aircraft Group 12 in Japan. The Corsairs launched from USS *Saipan* (CVL-48), flown by U.S. Marine Corps pilots who ferried the AUs ashore. Subsequently, Flotille 14.F flew from Bach Mai Airfield near Hanoi—a decade later an auxiliary MiG base.

With 25 pilots and aircraft, the squadron logged 1,422 sorties in the futile defense of Dien Bien Phu. Casualties amounted to two pilots and six aircraft, all attributable to Communist antiaircraft fire. After the armistice, the AU-1s were returned to the U.S. Navy in the Philippines while the F4U-7s were delivered aboard the light carrier *Bois de Belleau* (previously CVL-24), returning to Tunisia in July 1955.

Continuing warfare in Algeria resulted in commitment of three other Corsair squadrons to operations: Flotille 12.F, 15.F, and 17.F, as well as 14.F. The F4U-7s flew not only from Oran, Telergma, and Bizerte, but occasionally from the carrier *Arromanches*. Several pilots and aircraft were lost in Algeria while engaged in ground-support missions.

Some of the AU-1s which were returned to the U.S. Navy in 1955

*BuNo 129320, the third AU-1, over the Texas countryside. Of 111 built, all went to the Marine Corps for Korean combat or to the French for use in Indochina. (Fred Johnsen)*

were overhauled and sold to France in order to replace attrition in Algeria.

France's final Corsair combat occurred during early November 1956, when 14.F and 15.F flew in support of Anglo-French operations to keep the Suez Canal open. Three British and two French carriers were engaged, with 36 F4U-7s of Flotille 14.F and 15.F embarked in *Arromanches* and *Lafayette*. During this brief episode the commanding officer of 14.F was shot down over Cairo.

Last of the French F4U squadrons was Flotille 14.F in late 1964, as by then *Aeronaval* was taking delivery of a new generation of Vought fighters—the long-lived F-8E(FN) Crusader, which remains in service 32 years later.

Corsairs ended their front-line career in Latin America during the 1960s. The Argentine Navy flew F4U-5s circa 1958-1965 while Honduras and El Salvador Corsairs fought during the "Soccer War" of 1969. Honduras had acquired four F4U-4s and ten F4U-5s during 1956-1961 while El Salvador received FG-1Ds. During the eight-day conflict, the only recorded aerial victories were scored by a Honduran fighter pilot who shot down two Salvadoran Corsairs and a P-51D Mustang. They were probably the last air-to-air kills ever claimed by a piston-powered fighter.

*Developed from the XF4U-6 low-level fighter with the R-2800-83W single-stage engine, the AU-1 was a workhorse rather than the thoroughbred developed in the late 1930s. Despite 2,300 horsepower, the AU was rated at only 238 MPH at 9,500 feet, with a service ceiling of less than 20,000 feet. However, with immense payload and greater protection, its gross weight was nearly two and a half tons greater than the F4U-4. (SDAM)*

# THE ULTIMATE CORSAIR

**C**onventional wisdom sometimes falls short of historic fact, and such is the case with the F2G series—widely regarded as the ultimate Corsair. According to legend, the *kamikaze* crisis of late 1944 impelled the Navy and Goodyear Aircraft to undertake a crash program of producing a "super fighter" capable of meeting the suicide threat: a fast, powerful aircraft that could climb to altitude on short notice and intercept *kamikazes* before they smashed into their targets.

In fact, the F2G program was well underway when the first suiciders impacted American escort carriers in Leyte Gulf in October 1944.

With Vought devoted to building F4Us, Goodyear was the logical choice to produce the next model Corsair. Brewster Aircraft was shut down by the Navy following a series of management problems and production-line delays. The company produced only 735 Corsairs from June 1943 to July 1944—an average of just 56 per month. By comparison, in Goodyear's first year of building Corsairs the Akron, Ohio, plant turned out 75 per month, with a one-month high nearly twice Brewster's best effort.

BuAer informed Goodyear that the new Corsair should be designed and manufactured with three concepts in mind: greater rate of climb, higher top speed, and retention of as many FG-1 airframe components as possible. The latter was necessary if sufficient wartime production was to be attained.

Selected to power the new Corsair was a new Pratt & Whitney product: the R-4300-4, developing 3,500 horsepower. A huge engine for a fighter, the Wasp Major's 28 cylinders were arranged in four banks of seven to gain the 4,300 cubic inches of displacement. Because the Major was 15 inches longer and 1,300

*One of the original "Super Corsairs," a Goodyear XF2G-1 with a startling insignia yellow cowling to offset the standard dark gloss blue paint. With production limited to prototypes, the F2G series made its impression on aviation history in the civilian arena during postwar Thompson Trophy races. (SDAM)*

pounds heavier than the R-2800, Goodyear had to re-engineer the XF2G-1 for entirely new weight and balance figures in order to maintain a center of gravity.

Armament was reduced from six .50 calibers to four—essentially the same armament as the F4F-3 of 1940. However, it was considered adequate for destroying most Japanese aircraft still encountered in 1945. The new Corsair's offensive punch was increased with addition of two pylons for ordnance upwards of 1,600 pounds.

The F2G contract was inked on 22 March 1944 with first flight nine weeks later, on 31 May. However, early flight tests were conducted in FG-1s modified to accept the Wasp Major engine. These aircraft were given the factory designation EXF2G-1—a model unknown to the Navy to this day.

First flight of the prototype "real" XF2G-1 came on 15 October 1944, with Don Armstrong in the cockpit. Intimately involved with the "Super Corsair," Armstrong was an experienced test pilot who had previously worked at Curtiss and Douglas. At the end of that first F2G flight, Armstrong was asked by Goodyear vice president Karl Arnstein how the fighter performed. Impressed with the spectacular rate of climb, Armstrong enthusiastically replied, "It's a homesick angel!"

*Portside console of the Champlin F2G. Most prominent are the throttle quadrant with propeller and mixture controls, trim handles, fuel tank selector knob, and landing gear and flap actuators. (Fred Johnsen)*

*Instrument panel of BuNo 88454, the first of five F2G-1s, displayed at the Champlin Fighter Museum in Mesa, Arizona. Top row, L-R: radio compass, vertical speed, artificial horizon, turn and bank indicator, magnetic compass. Middle row: altimeter, gyro compass, airspeed indicator, and G meter. Bottom row: tachometer, manifold pressure, cylinder head temperature, and fuel gauges. (Fred Johnsen)*

*Decked out in a flashy white paint job with race number 99, NX63382, an FG-1D, shares the ramp with USAAF P-80s at the 1946 national air races. (SDAM)*

*Race number 74 (BuNo 88463) was flown by Cleland in 1947, then by Dick Becker, who dropped out on the third lap of the 1948 Thompson and was unable to start the next year. (Warren M. Bodie via SDAM)*

The F2G's initial climb rate of 4,400 feet per minute needs to be placed in context. Two of America's earliest operational jets were the Lockheed P-80A and Republic P-84B (both later designated F rather than P). The Shooting Star clocked 4,580 FPM and the Thunderjet 4,210, and not until the F-86A Sabre did an operational jet fighter substantially outclimb the late-war piston fighters.

Switching cockpits between the EX and XF models required attention to detail. As Armstrong recalled it, "The two aircraft looked comparable, but each had disparate characteristics and responded differently in flight. It was like a man with two lovers—sisters, almost identical, but not twins—and you damn well better remember which one you were with!"

Originally providing for 418 F2G-1s and ten dash twos, the contract was immediately cut back after VJ-Day, resulting in just five examples of each type. The XF2G-2 was the carrier version of the super Corsair, with folding wings, catapult fittings, and tailhook. Additionally, the dash two possessed an auxiliary rudder beneath the standard one for enhanced stability and improved control at high speed.

Despite the attempt at commonality of airframe parts, several changes were necessary over the FG-1. Besides a bigger, heavier engine, additional fuel also was required to maintain a 1,000-mile ferry range for the improved Corsair. With some 72 gallons extra internal fuel, the F2G's fuel system itself also was redesigned, with somewhat different cockpit controls. Consequently, the F2G received a beefed-up wing and

*Jim Landry's FG-1D taking off from Everett, Washington, in 1983. The owner decided to honor VF-17 by painting the Corsair as Tom Blackburn's "Big Hog," complete with a rare centerline fuel tank. Apart from a high-gloss paint job, civilian fixtures include advanced avionics such as UHF radios and DME gear. (Sharon Kaproth)*

center section, with reinforced horizontal stabilizers to withstand higher-G pullouts.

The R-4300 engine, an entirely new design over the R-2800, came with different induction, exhaust, supercharger, and intercooler controls which in turn altered some of the cockpit layout.

*A restored F4U-7 with wings folded. Noteworthy are the two 20MM cannon barrels protruding from the leading edge, and the Fowler type flaps at the trailing edge. The complex hydraulic system which controlled wing folding is well displayed in this view—a considerable engineering feat considering that the system had to retain both strength and reliability under repeated use. (Fred Johnsen)*

Most of the other changes similarly reflected the Wasp Major's influence. Goodyear designed an entirely new cowling, which featured a top-mounted air intake. And, as with the XF4U-1 of 1938, the 1944 F2G needed yet again a larger propeller to use the available power. A four-blade Hamilton-Standard "Super Hydromatic" propeller was employed.

The most distinctive visual difference of the F2G was its bubble canopy. Rearward vision, always something of a problem in the Corsair, finally was solved with an all-round plexiglass design similar to

*A complete rebuild of a Jim Landry's FG-1D underway at Everett, Washington, in the 1970s. The restorer has reduced the airframe to its production components, as the fuselage sits on the landing gear, minus the wings, tail, and engine. One wing on a jig is undergoing reskinning in the foreground. (Fred Johnsen)*

*The same aircraft with Pratt & Whitney R-2800 engine installed. Visible in the accessory section are the engine mount, oil tank, and cables for engine controls, as well as fuel and oil lines. Even in the 1970s, a Corsair was not an economical aircraft to operate. At about this time, circa 1975, the cost of replacing one bank of spark plugs for a 2800 was around $500. (Fred Johnsen)*

the P-47D. So similar, in fact, that Goodyear obtained the loan of one from Republic Aircraft.

Overall, the F2G was bigger and heavier than any previous Corsair variant:

| FG-1D | F4U-4 | F2G-2 |
| --- | --- | --- |
| | Empty weight | |
| 8,695 lbs | 9,205 lbs | 10,249 lbs |
| | Gross weight | |
| 12,039 lbs | 12,420 lbs | 13,346 lbs |

| | VMax | |
| --- | --- | --- |
| FG-1D | 425MPH/20,000 | |
| F4U-4 | 446 MPH/26,200 | |
| F2G-2 | 431 MPH/16,400 | |

| | Climb rate | |
| --- | --- | --- |
| 3,120 FPM | 3,870 FPM | 4,400 FPM |

| | Normal range | |
| --- | --- | --- |
| 1,015 SM | 1,005 SM | 1,190 SM |

| | Fuel (in US gals) | |
| --- | --- | --- |
| 237 | 234 | 309 |

Aeronautical engineers know that increasing the power available to an airframe improves climb rate more than top speed in level flight. And so it was with the F2G, which provided a 40% increase in low-altitude climb over the FG-1D, but barely five MPH more top speed. More importantly, the new model was actually 15 MPH slower than the standard F4U-4 while gaining just 14% better climb.

*N5588N, the Sohio-sponsored F2G-1 as race number 57. Pilot Ben McKillen enjoyed some success with this Super Corsair, placing third in the 1949 Thompson (387 MPH) and winning the shorter Tinnerman Trophy race (386 MPH) that same year. (SDAM)*

*Cook Cleland's all-white F2G-1 (BuNo 14693), race number 94, showing original clipped wingtips and modified cowling, circa 1948. In 1949 Cleland flew this airplane to victory in the Thompson Trophy Race at an average speed of 397 MPH. (SDAM)*

*The same airplane, N5590N, with later paint scheme before the span was reduced by a total of some four feet. Stability and roll rate problems required addition of "spoiler plates" on the tips to regain some of the control lost in the modification. The F2G was reported scrapped about 1955. (SDAM)*

Similarly, the F2G's 32% greater internal fuel over the F4U-4 (309 to 234 U.S. gallons) was mostly offset by the R-4350's voracious appetite, resulting in a "clean" ferry range of an additional 18%.

The F2G was 18% heavier than FG-1D; 11% heavier than F4U-4. But gross weight (the difference in payload) was 11% over the FG and just 7% greater than the dash four. In short, for a substantial increase in climb rate, the F2G offered no increase in top speed, no useful increase in payload, and only a small improvement in range.

Additionally, the Navy already had a screamer of a carrier interceptor well on the way by mid-1945. Grumman's F8F-1 Bearcat was nearly as fast as the F2G and climbed slightly better. In the dash two model, the scrappy little Grumman was faster than the F2G-2 with a nearly identical rate of climb. Armament was the same as the F2G, with four .50 calibers, though four 20mm cannon were planned. Two Bearcat squadrons were already operational, with one bound for WestPac when the war ended. Clearly, the super Corsair was no longer needed.

### RACERS AND WARBIRDS

Postwar closed-course air racing inevitably drew Corsairs, and in the 1946 Cleveland event, former SBD pilot Cook Cleland finished sixth in a fairly stock FG-1D. The next year's starting field involved four F2Gs, including three owned by Cleland. Even at this late date, details are hard to acquire, but evidently Cleland and his local Naval Air Reserve squadron convinced the Navy that "unofficial" support of the Super Corsairs would be good for promoting the service's image. Whatever the reasoning, it proved logical as Cleland won by six miles at the end of 300 miles of low-level racing with Dick Becker finishing second. Their average race speeds were 396 and 390 MPH, respectively. However,

*View upwards into a main mount wheel well. The hydraulic cylinders pivoting outward from each side controlled the two landing gear doors which, when shut with the leading-edge gear door, fully enclosed the gear leg, wheel and tire. This photo affords a particularly good view of the landing gear well's "plumbing" for hydraulic and fuel lines.* (Fred Johnsen)

four planes were destroyed and one pilot killed in a controversial event that nearly ended unlimited air racing in the U.S.

The next year Cleland and Becker were back in contention but both their F2Gs dropped out by the fifth of 20 laps. Cleland set a course record with 410 MPH on laps three and four, indicating that the F2G remained competitive but lacked stamina.

However, 1949 was the Corsair's glory year. Not only did Cleland repeat his 1946 victory, but Ron Puckett finished in second place and Ben McKillen in third—a clean sweep for the F2G. Cleland's Number 94 crossed the finish line averaging 397 MPH: amazing consistency after his 396 MPH speed two years before.

Also in the 1949 event, the 225-mile Tinnerman Trophy Race was won by McKillen while Puckett placed second in the 105-mile Sohio Trophy event at 386 and 384 MPH, respectively.

Tragically, more deaths marred the 1949 race, leading to withdrawal of corporate sponsorships. Combined with the Korean War in 1950, unlimited air racing disappeared in the United States until the first Reno event in 1964. Subsequent

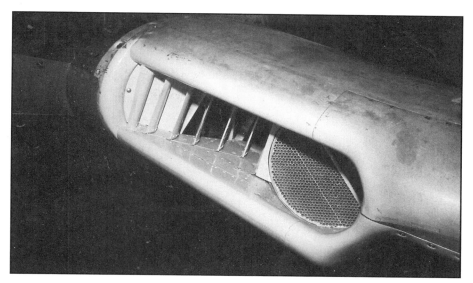

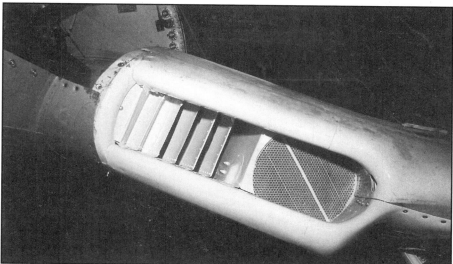

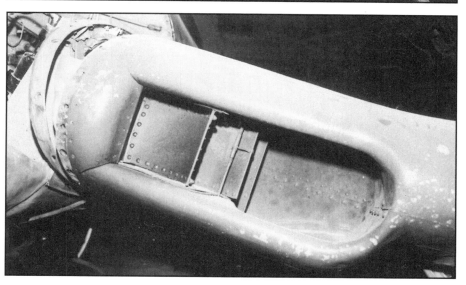

*Three views of the Corsair's distinctive wingroot-mounted oil cooler with shutter doors. In the top view they are fully open, permitting maximum cooling with the "honeycomb" cooler unit exposed to the airstream. In the second view the doors are partially closed, still providing air through the oil cooler. The third view shows the shutter doors fully closed, with the cooler itself protected from the slipstream. Depending upon position of the cooler doors and the aircraft's speed, the F4U emitted a distinctive high-pitched sound which became legendary as "whistling death." (Fred Johnsen)*

BuNo 97142, one of Bob Bean's F4U-4s at Mojave, California, circa 1977. Minus wings and tail feathers, formerly NRAB Seattle's "T-10," this much-abused Corsair wears the orange Reserve fuselage stripe over two-tone gray paint scheme common to 1960s naval aircraft. It subsequently went to the Pima County Air Museum a decade later. (Fred Johnsen)

races were dominated by modified P-51D Mustangs and F8F Bearcats with occasionally serious competition from Hawker Sea Furies, but Corsairs were notably absent.

Then in 1982 the "Super Corsair" reappeared, Phoenix-like, from oblivion. Fighter Rebuilders of Chino, California, attempted to replicate the F2G as closely as possible, with F4U-1, -4, and -5 airframe components and an R-4350 with Douglas Skyraider propeller and A-26 cowling. That first year pilot Steve Hinton logged a 362-MPH race speed to place fourth. He coaxed 413 MPH out of the composite Corsair the next year, moving up to third overall.

In 1985 Hinton took it all. He blazed around the 9.2-mile course at a stunning 438 MPH to capture the checkered flag. A Super Corsair was victorious for the first time in 36 years.

Thereafter, John Maloney and Kevin Ethridge campaigned Number One in ten more races between 1987 and 1994. The best finish in these events was Maloney's third place at Denver, Colorado, in 1990 before the plane was lost to an in-flight fire at Williams Field, Arizona, in 1994.

FG-1D port main mount. Under approx. 1,500 pounds of hydraulic pressure, the oleo leg extended downward to unlock, then rotated 90 degrees and retracted rearward into the wheel well, where two landing gear doors closed over the unit. When designed in the late 1930s, the Corsair's fully enclosed landing gear was a feature matched by very few other fighter aircraft. Such streamlining was in large part responsible for the F4U's speed. (Fred Johnsen)

# BIBLIOGRAPHY

Abrams, Richard. *F4U Corsair at War*. Scribners, New York, 1977.

--------. "The Night Fighters, VMF(N)-532." American Aviation Historical Society *Journal*. Spring 1973.

Armstrong, Don. *I Flew them First*. Champlin Press, Mesa, Arizona, 1955.

Blackburn, Tom. *The Jolly Rogers*. Orion, New York, 1989.

Brown, Eric M. *Duels in the Sky*. Naval Institute Press, Annapolis, 1988.

Dial, Jay Frank. *Profile 47: the Chance Vought F4U-1 Corsair*. Profile Publications, Leatherhead, UK, 1965.

--------. *Profile 150: the Chance Vought F4U-4 to F4U-7 Corsair*. Profile Publications, Windsor, UK, 1967.

Green, William. *Famous Fighters of the Second World War, 2nd Series*. MacDonald, London, 1962.

Guyton, Boone T. *Whistling Death*. Orion, New York, 1985.

Langeweische, Wolfgang. "What It's Like to Strap On an F4U" *Flying*, June 1977.

Sherrod, Robert. *History of Marine Corps Aviation in World War II*. Combat Forces Press, Washington, D.C., 1952.

Sturdivant, Ray. *British Naval Aviation. The Fleet Air Arm, 1917-1990*. Naval Institute Press, Annapolis, 1990.

Swanborough, Gordon, and Peter M. Bowers. *United States Navy Aircraft Since 1911*. Funk & Wagnalls, New York, 1968.

Tillman, Barrett. *Corsair: the F4U in WWII and Korea*. Naval Institute Press, Annapolis, 1979.

--------. "Korean War Combat Deployments." *The Hook*, Summer, 1989.

--------. "F4U-5: The Enigmatic Corsair." *The Hook*, Winter, 1992.

--------. "Five the Hard Way: Navy and Marine Corps Aces in a Day." *The Hook*, Fall 1993.

U.S. Navy. *Pilot's Handbook, Navy Models F4U-5, -5N, -5NL, -5P Aircraft*. (AN 01-45HD-1). Revised 1 April 1951. Reissued by Schiffer Military / Aviation History, Atglen, Pennsylvania, 1995.

--------. *Location and Allowance of Naval and Marine Corps Aircraft, August 1943; August 1945; July 1950; July 1953*.

--------. *United States Naval Aviation 1910-1970*. Washington, D.C., 1970.

Wagner, Ray. *American Combat Planes (3rd Edition)*. Doubleday, New York, 1982.

White, Graham. *Allied Aircraft Piston Engines of WWII*. Warrendale, Pennsylvania, 1995.

# SIGNIFICANT DATES

**FEBRUARY 1, 1938**
Navy design specification issued for new fighter.

**JUNE 11, 1938**
Vought receives Navy approval for XF4U-1.

**MAY 29, 1940**
First flight of XF4U-1.

**OCTOBER 1, 1940**
XF4U-1 logs record speed run of 405 MPH between Stratford and Hartford, Connecticut.

**JUNE 25, 1942**
First flight of a production F4U-1.

**SEPTEMBER, 1942**
First deliveries to a Marine Corps squadron, VMF-124, at Camp Kearney, California.

**OCTOBER, 1942**
First deliveries to a Navy squadron, VF-12 at San Diego.

**FEBRUARY 13, 1943**
First combat mission by VMF-124 from Guadalcanal.

**FEBRUARY 25, 1943**
First flight of Goodyear FG-1 Corsair.

**APRIL 26, 1943**
First flight of the Brewster F3A-1 Corsair.

**MAY 13, 1943**
1st Lt. K.A. Walsh becomes first Corsair ace.

**JUNE 1, 1943**
First Royal Navy Corsair unit, 1830 Squadron, formed at NAS Quonset Point, R.I.

**AUGUST 15-30, 1943**
Medal of Honor actions by 1st Lt. K.A. Walsh.

**OCTOBER 31, 1943**
First confirmed victory by a Navy Corsair, VF(N)-75 in the Solomon Islands.

**SEPTEMBER 1943-JANUARY 1944**
Medal of Honor actions by Maj. G. Boyington.

**NOVEMBER 1943-JANUARY 1944**
Medal of Honor actions by 1st Lt. R.A. Hanson.

**JANUARY 29, 1944**
First Corsair combat operations from U.S. carrier, USS *Enterprise*, by VF(N)-101.

**APRIL 3, 1944**
First Royal Navy combat missions from HMS *Victorious*.

**APRIL 19, 1944**
First flight of F4U-4XA.

**OCTOBER 15, 1944**
First flight of XF2G-1.

**DECEMBER 28, 1944**
First two Marine F4U squadrons begin carrier duty.

**AUGUST 9, 1945**
Victoria Cross action by Sub-Lt. R.H. Gray.

**APRIL 1946**
First flight of XF4U-5.

**JULY 3, 1950**
First Corsair missions of Korean War flown by Air Group Five, *USS Valley Forge*.

**DECEMBER 4, 1950**
Medal of Honor action by Lt.(jg) T.J. Hudner.

**DECEMBER 29, 1951**
First flight of AU-1.

**JULY 2, 1952**
First flight of F4U-7.

**DECEMBER 24, 1952**
Corsair production ends with the last F4U-7.

**JUNE 25, 1953**
Lt. G.P. Bordelon, VC-3, becomes last Corsair ace.

**DECEMBER 31, 1995**
Last Corsairs in U.S. operational use, VC-4.